SOS Help For Emotions:

Managing Anxiety, Anger, And Depression

SECOND EDITION

http://www.sosprograms.com

Self-Talk Causing Distress

"He has no right to talk to me that way. He must not, he should not have insulted me. He's a *§æ!±»! fool! What kind of *§æ!±»! person would say such a thing! I-can't-stand him saying that!"

> LEARN WHAT YOU ARE SAYING,
> WHEN YOU TALK TO YOURSELF.
> HERE LIES THE KEY TO YOUR EMOTIONS.

The main causes of our emotions and behavior are our thinking, our evaluation of events, and our silent self-talk statements.

Manage Anxiety, Anger, And Depression!

Read SOS Help For Emotions.
Manage your emotions before they manage you!

SOS Help For Emotions can help you to:
- **Know your self-talk**
- **Know your emotions**
- **Manage your emotions**
- **Manage your relationships**
- **Attain greater contentment**
- **Achieve your personal goals**
- **Enhance your emotional intelligence**

READ WHAT OTHERS ARE SAYING ABOUT SOS!

"Beautifully captures the spirit of Rational Emotive Behavior Therapy in concise, evocative, and humorous language. A gem of an introduction to REBT."
> – Albert Ellis, Ph.D., President of Albert Ellis Institute and author of *A Guide to Rational Living*.

"SOS is a beautiful work! The use of cartoons, figures, and illustrations is quite engaging."
> – Donald Beal, Ph.D., Associate Professor of Psychology, Eastern Kentucky University.

"It's spectacular! SOS is the best self-help book on Rational Emotive Behavior Therapy that I have seen."
> – Raymond DiGiuseppe, Ph.D., Director of Professional Education at Albert Ellis Institute and Professor of Psychology at St. John's University.

by Lynn Clark, Ph.D.

SOS Help For Emotions: Managing Anxiety, Anger, And Depression. Second Edition

English edition	SOS Programs & Parents Press
Turkish edition	Evrim Yaymevi ve Tic.Ltd. Co.
Korean edition	Kyoyuk-Kwahak-Sa, Ltd.
Chinese edition	Beijing Normal University Press

SOS Parenting Programs

SOS Help For Parents: A Practical Guide For Handling Common Everyday Behavior Problems. Third Edition

English edition	SOS Programs & Parents Press
Spanish edition	SOS Programs & Parents Press
Korean edition	Kyoyuk-Kwahak-Sa, Ltd.
Chinese edition	Beijing Normal University Press
Chinese edition	Taiwan, Psychological Co., Ltd.
Turkish edition	Evrim Yaymevi ve Tic.Ltd. Co.
Hungarian edition	Budapest, Pedagogia Szervezet
Icelandic edition	University of Iceland
Arabic edition	Yousef Abuhmaiden, Alkerak, Jordan

> Visit our website and see video examples
> of SOS parenting methods in English
> & Spanish. Also, download complimentary
> copies of SOS materials at
> http://**www.sosprograms.com**

The Video SOS Help For Parents, education program

English edition (DVD & VHS)	SOS Programs & Parents Press
Spanish edition (DVD & VHS)	SOS Programs & Parents Press
Hungarian edition	Budapest, Pedagogia Szervezet
Icelandic edition	University of Iceland

How To Use Time-Out Effectively, audio program

Child Management Skills Test (CMST)

SOS Help For Professionals, materials kit

Time-Out Parent Inventory (TOPI), Record Form and Manual

SOS Help For Parents: A Practical Guide For Handling Common Everyday Behavior Problems

English SOS

Spanish SOS

Turkish SOS

Chinese SOS
Beijing Normal University

Korean SOS

Chinese SOS
Taiwan

Hungarian SOS

Arabic SOS

Icelandic SOS

SOS Help For Emotions:
Managing Anxiety, Anger, And Depression

English
SOS Help For Emotions

Turkish
SOS Help For Emotions

Chinese
SOS Help For Emotions

Korean
SOS Help For Emotions

SOS

Help For Emotions:

Managing Anxiety, Anger, And Depression

SECOND EDITION

Lynn Clark, Ph.D.

SOS Programs & Parents Press
PO Box 2180
Bowling Green, KY. 42102-2180 U.S.A.
http://**www.sosprograms.com**

SOS Help For Emotions:
Managing Anxiety, Anger, And Depression

SECOND EDITION

Copyright © 2002 by Lynn Clark

With 2005 Revisions

Library of Congress Cataloging-in-Publication Data

Clark, Lynn, date.
    SOS help for emotions : managing anxiety, anger, and depression / Lynn Clark--2nd ed.
     p. cm.
    Includes bibliographical references and indexes.
    ISBN-10: 0-935111-52-2   ISBN-13: 978-0-935111-52-1
     1. Emotions. 2. Emotions--Problems, exercises, etc.
    I. Title: Help for emotions. II. Title

    BF561.C57 2001
    152.4--dc21

                              2001052374

Printed in the United States of America
Published by: SOS Programs & Parents Press
               Post Office Box 2180
               Bowling Green, KY 42102-2180 USA
               Telephone: 270-842-4571
               Toll free in USA: 1-800-576-1582
               Fax: 270-796-9194
               www.sosprograms.com

20 19 18 17 16 15 14 13 12 11 10 9 8 7 6 5 4

Publisher's Note

WARNING

This book is designed to provide information in regard to the subject matter covered. It is sold with the understanding that the publisher and author are not engaged in rendering psychological, medical, or other professional services.

Resolving emotional problems is sometimes very difficult. If expert assistance is needed, seek the services of a competent professional. Chapter 11 describes how to obtain professional help.

Mental Health Professionals often ask clients to read SOS in conjunction with counseling or therapy.

DEDICATION

To Carole, Eric, and Todd

ACKNOWLEDGMENTS

SOS Help For Emotions is grounded in cognitive behavior therapy. I am especially indebted to Albert Ellis, the grandfather of cognitive behavior therapy who has made profound contributions to the art and science of psychotherapy for over 45 years. I'm grateful to Dr. Ellis for reviewing and critiquing an early draft of Chapter Two, a core chapter. Dr. Ellis, who emphasizes the importance that humor plays in therapy and emotional adjustment, kindly gave permission to use the cartoon illustration in Chapter 13.

Ray DiGiuseppe, Director of Professional Education at Albert Ellis Institute of Rational Emotive Behavior Therapy and Professor of Psychology at St. John's University, reviewed the manuscript and contributed ideas in order to improve it. Don Beal, Associate Professor of Psychology at Eastern Kentucky University, also helped to improve the manuscript by reviewing it. The comments and recommendations of these practicing therapists make *SOS Help For Emotions* more useful and interesting.

Carole Clark, Eric Clark, and Todd Clark read and critiqued each of the many manuscript drafts and illustrations. They made many helpful suggestions regarding writing style and clarity of concepts. Todd kept my two computers running which were necessary for this project.

Individuals at Western Kentucky University who contributed to SOS include Libby Jones, Ned Kearny, Clint Layne, Judy Pierce, and Bill Pfohl. Cindy Oetting and Terry Oetting reviewed various chapters.

Copyreading and proofreading were done by Mary Dillingham. Betty Kerby and Joanie Powers helped by evaluating and suggesting improvements to the illustrations and art work.

John Robb, drew the illustrations for *SOS Help For Emotions* as well as for my earlier book, *SOS Help For Parents*. John had felt that the message of SOS was valuable and came out of retirement to draw its illustrations. I was saddened to learn that he died in his sleep. John's daughter, Kathy Robb Parks, a commercial artist living in Chula Vista, California, completed the few remaining illustrations.

SOS readers, including mental health professionals, have offered many reactions regarding the first edition and contributed ideas for the second edition.

I'm indebted to all the individuals mentioned above who contributed in so many ways.

"I used to believe that others must never put me down and if they did, I felt worthless and I-couldn't-stand-it. Believing that got me into a lot of fights! I'm working on accepting myself and ignoring what others say or think."

Anger is often triggered by threats to our self-worth or self-esteem. Our beliefs and self-talk primarily cause our anger rather than what others do or say.

Some people with an anger problem place a positive value on toughness and aggression. As adults, they are at high risk for emotional maladjustment.

CONTENTS

Part Two
MANAGING OUR EMOTIONS

SOS

Help For Emotions:

Managing Anxiety, Anger, And Depression

SECOND EDITION

http://www.sosprograms.com

Self-Talk And Beliefs Causing Anxiety

"I'd like to ask her for a date, but I'm afraid she might turn me down. If she turns me down, it would be awful, I'd be worthless, and I-couldn't-stand-it!"

YOUR SELF-TALK AND BELIEFS
MAINLY DETERMINE
YOUR FEELINGS AND BEHAVIOR

INTRODUCTION

SOS Help For Emotions is your guide for handling a wide variety of common emotional problems. We'll look at questions and at solutions to problems such as the following:

Emotional Problems People Face

- Does seventeen year-old Janet absolutely need a 100% perfect body in order to have healthy self-esteem?

- Is there an alternative to either expressing anger or holding it in?

- How can Maria manage her intense anxiety so that she is able to give her speech at school?

- Am I responsible for my own emotions or are other people and unpleasant events in the world responsible?

- How can I more effectively cope with anger, resentment, worry, and frustration?

- Do people feel more "stressed out" by burdens that others place on them or by burdens that they place on themselves?

- What are panic disorder, agoraphobia, social phobia, obsessive-compulsive disorder, and bipolar disorder?

- How can getting fired from a valued job cause Barb to be clinically depressed for months afterward?

- What can Joshua do about his panic attacks?

- Tyler wants to ask Jessica for a date. How can he control his anxiety in order to do so?

Why I Wrote *SOS Help For Emotions*

My primary goal in writing SOS Help For Emotions is to help people to better manage anxiety, anger, depression, and other unpleasant feelings. As a result of repeatedly applying SOS methods and principles, you can expect to more effectively handle life's problems and frustrations and to better manage relationships with others. In addition, you will experience increased contentment and gain improved ability to set and achieve realistic goals.

SOS teaches principles and self-help methods from the cognitive behavior therapy perspective (and especially from rational emotive behavior therapy). In *SOS Help For Emotions,* I have attempted to clearly explain these self-help methods in an interesting and engaging way. This is why I have made extensive use of illustrations. I wrote *SOS Help For Emotions* because I couldn't find another book like it.

Who Can Benefit From SOS?

SOS is intended for both adults and older teens who desire to achieve increased self-knowledge and greater control over their unpleasant emotions.

I wrote SOS for people interested in how positive emotional change can occur, for clients of therapists, and for the many people who choose not to seek out a counselor, but who want to assist themselves by studying self-help materials. Individuals who want to increase those abilities comprising emotional intelligence, will find SOS useful in doing so.

Most counselors recommend self-help books to their clients. I also wrote SOS for counselors who want to accelerate therapy by assigning reading materials to their clients in order to increase self-understanding and positive change. SOS can be used in a variety of programs and settings serving adults and youth. Many of these programs and settings are listed in Chapter 13 (Information For Counselors).

Acts of anger and violence are becoming more and more common in contemporary society. What should we tell our youth to do with their anger, to hold it in or to let it out? Educators, school counselors, parents, and helping professionals are responsible for helping others deal with emotional and relationship problems. They will find SOS methods and principles to be useful when helping adults or youth to understand the cause of their upset feelings and what they can do to better manage their emotions.

Undergraduate and graduate students studying therapy and counseling need to learn cognitive behavior therapy. *SOS Help For Emotions* provides a clear, easy-to-understand introduction.

The Best Way To Use This Book

Read SOS and practice its exercises and recommendations. At the end of each chapter is a section called "Main Points To Remember." These are the most important ideas and recommendations contained in that chapter.

Throughout SOS, I occasionally ask you to complete various exercises to check your understanding of the self-help methods that you are reading about.

Chapter 12 has four sets of quizzes and exercises which correspond to the four parts of SOS. After reading Chapters One, Two, and Three (Part One of SOS), turn to Chapter 12 and complete the first set of quizzes and exercises. You will get valuable feedback about your understanding of these first three chapters, and you will understanding of these first three chapters, and you will gain experience applying SOS methods and principles to your life. There also are quizzes and exercises over the last three parts of SOS. They are included in Chapter 12 as well.

A number of *Guidepost Sayings* appear throughout SOS. These *SOS Sayings* are especially important. Select those which are most significant to you and post copies where you will see them several times a day!

SOS Guidepost Saying

MANAGE ANXIETY, ANGER, AND DEPRESSION
BEFORE
THEY MANAGE YOU!

SOS Help For Emotions is based on my university teaching and professional practice as a clinical psychologist, the experience of my colleagues, my own personal experiences, and the conclusions of numerous research studies on therapy.

By understanding and applying the SOS program, you can expect to learn useful self-help methods, to gain insights for improving your thoughts and feelings, and to become more successful in attaining your goals.

Let's begin with Chapter One, *Achieving Contentment and Our Goals!*

Technical Talk: The foundation for SOS is rational emotive behavior therapy and cognitive behavior therapy. References for over 500 outcome research studies on rational emotive behavior therapy are listed at <www.rebt.org>.

Part One

UNDERSTANDING
OUR
EMOTIONS

Chapter 1

Achieving Contentment And Our Goals

MEETING THE SABER-TOOTHED TIGER

Our "fight or flight response" and emotions such as fear enabled our prehistoric ancestors to survive in a dangerous world. When meeting a saber-toothed tiger, flight was usually the best response!

Fighting The Snake

It was nighttime and I was crawling under my house with a flashlight, intent on moving a TV line from one room to another. Distracted by a maze of pipes, lines, and bugs, I crawled right up to a snake! I froze and panicked at seeing its two eyes, and said to myself, "*It's a snake!*" My breathing became rapid and my heart started pounding. As I raised my flashlight to hit the snake, I said to myself, "*If I miss the snake I'll probably break my flashlight, and then the snake and I'll be in the dark together.*" I shuddered, reached for a pipe, and then struck at the snake.

My wife and son, on the floor above me and hearing the struggle, called down, "*What are you doing?*" I replied, "*I'm recovering from just killing a snake,*" to which my son yelled back, "*Be careful dad; where there's one snake, there might be more!*" Another series of chills went over me as I cautiously looked around. After assuring myself that my immediate area was free of snakes, I finished moving the TV line.

When I returned to the safety of my house, I thought about my emotion of fear and my fight or flight reaction. My emotional response to the snake was essentially the same response to dangerous situations experienced by our ancestors many ages ago.

As I thought about the snake, I also felt some regret for my actions since the snake hadn't caused our encounter. I had experienced a "fight or flight response." What was important, however, was that I now felt safe.

Contentment And Our Goals

We all want to be happy and achieve our goals. However, anxiety, anger, depression, and other unpleasant emotions cause distress interfering with our contentment, health, relationships, and other life goals. The anxiety I experienced under my house almost prevented me from staying until I moved the TV line.

The purpose of this book is to help you to decrease and manage your anxiety, anger, and depression and to help you to increase your contentment in daily living. As a result, you can be more successful in attaining your goals, enjoying life more, experiencing better relationships, and having better health.

Unpleasant and out-of-control emotions not only reduce our pleasure in day-to-day living, but block us from attaining our goals. Unbridled emotions can also damage our health. Continuing anger and impatience can cause us to be vulnerable to a variety of cardiovascular problems. For example, a surge of anger can spike our blood pressure, causing a blood vessel to burst leading to a stroke. In many other ways, intense unpleasant emotions damage our bodies and adversely change our lives.

Individuals vary greatly in their vulnerability and response to stress. Some people experience mildly stressful events and become more upset than others who experience severely stressful events. Shortly we will be exploring why individuals differ in their emotional response to stress.

Let's examine more closely the nature of our emotions. We'll be considering contentment, anxiety, anger, and depression.

Four Core Emotions

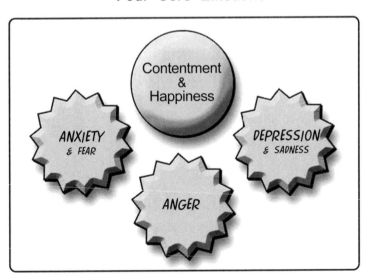

Our four core emotions are contentment, anxiety, anger, and depression.

The Four Core Emotions

What are emotions? *Emotions are complex feelings with mental, physical, and behavioral components.* *Mentally,* we experience our emotions and feelings as pleasant or unpleasant. *Physically,* we experience them as strong awareness or tension. *Behaviorally,* we experience our feelings and emotions as an impulse to act.

When I encountered the snake, mentally I evaluated the event as unpleasant and threatening. Physically, my breathing and heart rate increased. Behaviorally, I felt a strong impulse to act: fight or flight.

Our four basic emotions are fear, anger, sadness, and enjoyment or contentment (Goleman, 1995). Sustained fear experienced in many different situations becomes anxiety. Anger is a strong feeling of displeasure and antagonism. Lasting, enduring sadness becomes depression. *Contentment is a sense of well-being and pleasant feelings without much anxiety, anger, and depression.* SOS Help For Emotions focuses on these emotions of anxiety (sustained fear), anger, depression (sustained sadness), and contentment. Let's now consider emotional intelligence and how it relates to our emotions.

Emotional Intelligence

Just as people vary in their general intelligence, they vary in their emotional intelligence. *Emotional intelligence is the ability to understand and manage one's emotions* (Goleman, 1995).*

High intelligence and a good education don't guarantee you control over your emotions or success in life. Intense emotions and a low frustration tolerance, if not managed well, can defeat you.

---

* Technical Talk: Emotional intelligence is closely related to wisdom, insight, and judgment. Social intelligence includes understanding others' emotions and behavior and managing relationships.

Success and recognition from his peers were central goals for John, a young Ph.D. psychologist. Emotionally vulnerable to criticism, he once became so involved in defending his research at a convention that he punched another psychologist in the nose. His defensiveness, lack of emotional control, and criticism of his colleagues and department chairperson eventually cost him his job. John is an example of a bright, well-educated person whose lack of emotional insight and poor management of emotions defeated his goals.

Poorly managing our emotions can create severe problems in our relationships. Angrily screaming, "I hate you," to a child or other loved one damages our relationship with that person.

Your emotional intelligence likely contributes more to successful and enjoyable living, than your general intelligence. *Since emotional intelligence is learned rather than inherited, it can be improved.* In the following chapters, SOS teaches specific methods enabling you to better handle your emotions. Now, let's consider the components of emotional intelligence.

Five abilities comprise our emotional intelligence (Goleman, 1995). These abilities include:
- Knowing our emotions
- Managing our emotions
- Recognizing emotions in others
- Managing relationships with others
- Motivating ourselves to achieve our goals

Let's briefly look at each of these parts of emotional intelligence. The first ability, *knowing our emotions*, is self-awareness, understanding our central feelings, and being able to name our emotions. Knowing our emotions also means being aware of our silent self-talk statements and automatic thoughts accompanying our emotions and moods.

The second ability, *managing our emotions*, is highly dependent on knowing our emotions, our automatic thoughts, and our silent self-talk statements. *Learning to more effectively manage our emotions is critical in successful living and is the primary goal of SOS.* Many people attempt to soothe their emotions by overeating, drinking alcohol, taking "recreational" drugs, and overworking. These maladaptive ways to calm ourselves lead to increased emotional and relationship problems.

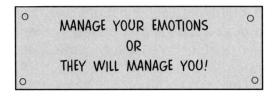

MANAGE YOUR EMOTIONS
OR
THEY WILL MANAGE YOU!

Effectively managing our emotions includes:

- soothing and calming ourselves when upset
- practicing self-control
- managing anger
- controlling impulses
- expressing emotions at the right time and place
- avoiding sustained anxiety, anger, and depression
- handling inevitable defeats and setbacks in life
- preventing negative emotions from dominating our judgment and problem solving

Two additional ingredients for managing our emotions, particularly important in SOS, are:

- tolerating frustration
- accepting and valuing ourselves

LEARN TO SOOTHE YOUR EMOTIONS

Five Steps To Emotional Intelligence
And Three Unhealthy Emotions To Manage

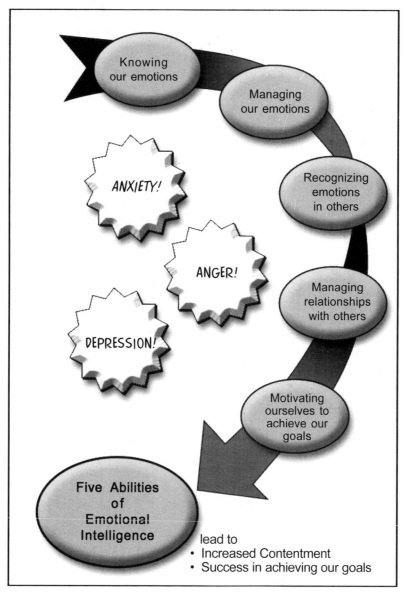

Enhance your emotional intelligence and avoid trapping yourself in the unhealthy emotions of anxiety, anger, and depression.

Recognizing emotions in others is the ability to read and understand another's feelings and intentions. Stephen Covey, in *The Seven Habits Of Highly Effective People*, advises us, "Seek first to understand, then to be understood." Dale Carnegie, in *How To Win Friends And Influence People*, recommends, "Be a good listener; encourage others to talk about themselves." Recognizing emotions in others depends on attentive listening and encouraging others to express their thoughts and feelings. Empathy and compassion are extensions of the ability to recognize another's feelings.

Managing relationships with others is the fourth part of emotional intelligence. People who excel in this ability handle relationships smoothly, connect with others, are appropriately assertive, can negotiate solutions to conflict and mutual problems, and can handle difficult people. Managing relationships is highly dependent on knowing our emotions, managing our emotions, and recognizing emotions in others.

Motivating ourselves to achieve attainable goals is the final part of emotional intelligence. This ability of emotional intelligence involves planning, persistence, delaying gratification, tolerating frustration, resisting impulsive behavior, recovering from defeats and setbacks in life, and finding satisfaction in current activities. Motivating ourselves to achieve our goals, of course, is dependent on knowing and managing our emotions.

Five Abilities Of Emotional Intelligence

- Knowing our emotions
- Managing our emotions
- Recognizing emotions in others
- Managing relationships with others
- Motivating ourselves to achieve our goals

Job success, in our competitive and demanding economy, is increasingly related to the five abilities comprising our emotional intelligence. Initiating and successfully maintaining intimate relationships is highly dependent on our emotional intelligence as is avoiding relationships harmful to us.

Thomas Edison's Emotional Intelligence

Thomas Edison eventually invented the electric light bulb after many years of effort and after failing 1,000 times. Which two of the five abilities of emotional intelligence did he most strongly demonstrate?
1. Knowing our emotions
2. Managing our emotions
3. Recognizing emotions in others
4. Managing relationships with others
5. Motivating ourselves to achieve our goals

For the answer to this question see the footnote on a following page.

SINCE EMOTIONAL INTELLIGENCE
IS LEARNED
RATHER THAN INHERITED,
IT CAN BE IMPROVED

The Origin Of Our Emotions

What causes our emotions? Where do they come from? Powerful emotions enabled our prehistoric ancestors to survive in an "eat or be eaten" world. These same emotions and the brain centers housing them have been handed down genetically for countless generations. We still experience these primitive emotions even though there are no longer saber-toothed tigers in our lives.

High levels of tension, alertness, anxiety, and aggression as well as an instant fight or flight response helped our ancestors to survive saber-toothed tigers and other physical dangers. But in our modern world, without daily life and death struggles, these powerful emotions can cause problems in adapting to the world and smoothly relating to other people.

Specific primitive centers in our brain markedly influence our emotions. However, our use of language and higher brain centers can greatly influence and override our more primitive brain centers. The main influences on our emotions and behavior are thinking, our evaluation of events, and our silent self-talk statements.

Your particular genetic makeup does influence your tendency to be calm or excitable, but only to a small extent. Childhood experiences and current emotional support from people close to you help to influence your emotional calm. Various physical conditions (illness, lack of sleep, poor nutrition) can predispose you to be easily upset. However, for the vast majority of us, these factors do not significantly determine our level of contentment or freedom from anxiety, anger, or depression.

Thomas Edison's Emotional Intelligence – In my opinion, Edison most strongly demonstrated emotional intelligence ability #5 (Motivating ourselves to achieve our goals) and #2 (Managing our emotions). He needed to manage his feelings of frustration in order to persevere in attaining his goals. Most people would have given up.

Our emotions are largely, but not entirely, controlled by our beliefs, the way we think about problems, and our silent self-talk. If physical conditions and illness are predisposing you to experience unpleasant emotions, get medical help for those physical conditions which can be changed. Also, learn and practice the methods presented in SOS. *Our irrational patterns of thinking are like bad habits; both are self-defeating and difficult to change.*

```
YOU CAN'T MANAGE YOUR LIFE
UNTIL
YOU MANAGE YOUR EMOTIONS
```

Can Emotions Damage Our Health?

Yes! It is well accepted by physicians, psychiatrists, and psychologists that stressful events, emotional distress, and our evaluation of unpleasant events profoundly affect our health (Gatchel & Blanchard, 1993; American Psychiatric Association, 1994). Psychological factors can initiate or intensify physical damage to our body.* The damage can be temporary or permanent. However, there are many reports of people recovering from certain kinds of serious illnesses by altering their mental outlook and emotional state.

What is stressful for one person might not be stressful for another. As we'll learn in the next chapter, our interpretation and evaluation of unpleasant events will primarily determine how emotionally upsetting those events are.

---

*In *Emotional Intelligence* (1995, pp. 324-328), Goleman lists a number of studies on mind and medicine. Anxiety, anger, and depression can lead to a wide variety of physical disorders.

How can emotional stress harm our bodies? Emotional stress can cause increased muscle tension leading to teeth grinding, tension headaches, and other kinds of muscle pain. Blood vessel spasms in the brain can cause migraine headaches.

Anger and fear cause substances to be released into our blood which increase the chance of clots forming. Receiving bad news can raise blood pressure to dangerous levels. Increased blood pressure and blood which clots quickly helped our prehistoric ancestors survive encounters with saber-toothed tigers. However, in our modern sedentary world, increased blood pressure and quickly clotting blood endanger our health. Physical processes which once helped our ancestors to survive can kill us.

Emotional turmoil can suppress our immune system, causing us to suffer from viral and bacterial infections. Stress can cause changes in the lining of the nose, throat, sinuses, and lungs leading to frequent or chronic infections. Several types of skin rash and hair loss have psychological causes.

Emotional distress can stimulate the stomach to secrete too much acid which can lead to heartburn and gastritis. Nausea, vomiting, diarrhea, and constipation can be brought on by emotional problems. It is well-known that eating disorders such as bulimia and anorexia have psychological causes.

Poor understanding and management of our emotions can undermine our contentment, relationships, and goals as well as harm our health. Use SOS to help you to better manage your emotions and life!

YOU CAN'T MANAGE RELATIONSHIPS
UNTIL
YOU MANAGE YOUR EMOTIONS

Poorly Managed Anxiety, Anger, And Depression Contribute To Emotional Problems And Disorders

Anxiety related problems and disorders:
generalized anxiety disorder
panic attacks and disorders
a•gor•a•pho•bia
social phobia
social anxiety disorder
specific phobias
obsessive-compulsive disorder (OCD)
obsessions, compulsions
hy•po•chon•dri•a•sis
adjustment disorder with anxiety

Anger related problems and disorders:
anger at self, others, or the world.
short temper, snapped, went off on
rage reactions
defensiveness, irritableness
conduct disorder
oppositional defiant disorder
intermittent explosive disorder

Depression related problems and disorders:
clinical depression
dys•thy•mic disorder
major depressive disorder
bipolar disorder (also called manic-depressive)
cy•clo•thy•mic disorder
adjustment disorder with depression
low self-esteem, low self-acceptance

Problems-in-living often result from mixtures of high levels of anxiety, anger, depression and and from various other factors. Common problems include: conflict in relationships (job, family, parenting), eating disorders, substance abuse, sleep disorder, procrastination, low frustration tolerance, resistence to being responsible for one's self and family.

Main Points To Remember:

• Anxiety, anger, depression, and other unpleasant emotions cause mental and physical distress and can interfere with our contentment, health, relationships, and goals in life.*

• For successful and enjoyable living, our emotional intelligence (understanding and managing our emotions) matters more than our general intelligence.

• Since emotional intelligence is learned rather than inherited, it can be improved.

• Job success in our competitive and demanding economy is increasingly related to the five abilities comprising our emotional intelligence.

• Our thinking, personal evaluation of events, and silent self-talk statements mainly control our emotions and behavior.

• The goal of SOS is to help you manage your anxiety, anger, depression, and other emotions so that you are both more contented and successful in attaining your goals.

```
○                                                                    ○
        LISTEN TO WHAT PEOPLE TELL YOU.
     LISTEN CLOSELY TO WHAT YOU TELL YOURSELF!
○                                                                    ○
```

---

* *The Merck Manual Of Medical Information: Second Home Edition* at <www.merck.com/pubs/mmanual> is my favorite book and website for information on health problems and treatments. The website is a valuable free resource, although somewhat technical. For information on a variety of medications go to <www.drugdigest.org>.

Chapter 2

ABC Origin Of Our Emotions And Behavior

ABC's OF OUR EMOTIONS

We need to learn and practice the *ABC's Of Our Emotions.*

A's are *activating events* or unpleasant situations which we encounter. B's are our *beliefs and self-talk statements* or what we silently tell ourselves about these activating events. C's are our *consequences*, both emotional and behavioral. These consequences include anxiety, anger, depression, other unpleasant feelings, and our behaviors.

Our emotions and behaviors result mainly from our beliefs and self-talk statements rather than from the actual unpleasant events and situations in our lives.

SOS teaches us how to improve our emotions and behaviors. It does this by using the self-help methods from

The author expresses appreciation to Albert Ellis for reviewing and critiquing a draft of this chapter.

cognitive therapy and rational emotive behavior therapy. This approach to helping people was pioneered by Dr. Albert Ellis and other therapists to help their clients cope with anxiety, anger, depression, and other troublesome emotions and behaviors.

Understanding and practicing self-help methods from rational emotive behavior therapy (REBT) will improve our emotional intelligence, enabling us to live more successfully and enjoyably.*

From the prior chapter, we learned that emotional intelligence consists of:
- Knowing our emotions
- Managing our emotions
- Recognizing emotions in others
- Managing relationships with others
- Motivating ourselves to achieve our goals

For happy, effective living, *our emotional intelligence may matter more than our general intelligence.*

R	E	B	T
Rational	Emotive	Behavior	Therapy
(thinking)	(feeling)	(behaving)	(help)

REBT is help for thinking, feeling, and behaving.

What is *rational emotive behavior therapy*? This therapy focuses on improving three realms of our lives: rational, emotive, and behavioral. **Rational** means thinking, reasoning, and cognition. **Emotive** means emotions, mood, and feelings. **Behavior** is the behaving and acting part of you. People spend their lives thinking, feeling, and behaving. Most of the time, many people engage in these activities happily and successfully. Unfortunately, some

---

* REBT is the usual abbreviation for rational emotive behavior therapy. However, most people find the initials REB-T easier to remember. REB-T sounds like the beginning letters in REBEL, with a T added at the end. Sound out REB-T yourself!

people spend much of their time *thinking crookedly* (irrationally), and as a result, feel miserable, and behave in self-defeating ways. A desirable objective is to spend the vast majority of our days, months, and years feeling contented and successful.

THE THINKER*

Rational emotive behavior therapy, or rational emotive therapy for short, was originated by psychologist, Dr. Albert Ellis, in the 1950's. Current researchers and therapists continue to refine REBT and expand its applications for helping people. Ellis is considered by contemporary psychotherapists to be the grandfather of cognitive behavior therapy, a research-based therapy recognized and practiced internationally (Corey, 2000).**

---

* *"If you are pained ..."* is by Marcus Aurelius Antoninus, Roman philosopher (about 180 AD). Auguste Rodin of France, created the sculpture known as "The Thinker."

** Technical talk: Cognitive Behavior Therapy (CBT) includes Rational Emotive Behavior Therapy (REBT of Ellis), Cognitive Therapy (CT of Beck), and Cognitive Behavior Modification (CBM of Meichenbaum). For more information about REBT see, *Information For Counselors*, Chapter 13.

Don't let the long name of rational emotive behavior therapy concern you. REBT is practical, straight forward, easily understood, and effective in helping people manage their emotions. It enables you to take responsibility for your emotions and to stop blaming other people, the world, or misfortunes for your continuing anger or depression. For this reason, REBT is sometimes called the "no cop-out," no excuses therapy. I view rational emotive behavior therapy as the most valuable self-help therapy for emotions offered by psychologists and psychiatrists.

From SOS, you can expect to learn useful methods and insights for improving your thinking and feeling, as well as to become more successful in attaining your goals. Let's begin by learning the *ABC's Of Our Emotions*.

Our beliefs and views of the world determine our emotions, feelings, and behavior. Epictetus, a Greek philosopher who lived 2,000 years ago (about 55-135 AD), announced, *"People are disturbed not by things, but by the views which they take of them."* (Ep·ic·te'·tus)

ABC's Of Our
Thinking, Feeling, And Behaving

Our emotional upsetness is caused largely, but not entirely, by our beliefs and silent self-talk statements about events and situations rather than by the actual events and situations themselves. The ABC's of rational emotive behavior therapy illustrate the primary cause of our emotions.

A's are the activating events, actual events, or assumed sources of our stress. The A's include locking ourselves out of our car, receiving a "D" on a test, being stood up for a date, failing to get an expected promotion, and experiencing the many other inevitable disappointments and hard knocks of life. When you attempt to describe a past activating event to yourself, describe the event as video camera would record it and play it back.

What Are Activating Events?

- Activating events activate, stimulate, and awaken our thinking, beliefs, and silent self-talk statements. They are the adversities, frustrations, and stressors in our lives.

- Activating events can be in the past, present, or future (anticipated).

- Activating events can be real or imagined.

- An activating event can be a single isolated situation or a continuing unpleasant happening or disappointment.

- An activating event can be a bad event that did occur or a good event that didn't occur (a disappointment).

In addition to current events, *A's can also include thoughts of past events* such as the memory of being rejected by someone you loved or remembering a humiliating experience from your adolescence. In addition to memories of situations, *A's can include our thoughts about future, anticipated events or situations* such as planning to ask our boss for a raise or waiting in the doctor's office for an injection of antibiotic. *Activating events are situations which you remember or currently experience, or future events which concern you.*

Why are A's called activating events? A's are activating events because they activate, stimulate, and awaken our thinking, our system of rational and irrational beliefs, our silent self-talk statements, and our internal dialogue.

Individuals continually engage in inner speech, internal dialogue, automatic sentences, or self-talk with themselves. These self-talk statements are nearly automatic and are at a low-level of awareness. With this internal dialogue, we debate different courses of possible action and determine our feelings and emotional reactions to events and situations.

B's are our beliefs and silent self-talk statements, what we tell ourselves about activating events and situations. There are two major types of beliefs and self-talk. The first, *rational beliefs and self-talk, are self-helping, coping, and adaptive statements which lead to emotional health.* The second, *irrational beliefs and self-talk, are self-harming, self-defeating, maladaptive, internal statements which lead to emotional upsetness.**

Irrational beliefs lead to anxiety, anger, depression and to a feeling of not being in control of our emotions. Rational beliefs lead to <u>less</u> <u>disturbed</u> emotions such as concern, displeasure, annoyance, or sadness. Also, rational beliefs help us to cope more effectively, to get more of what we want in life, and to gain more contentment. The language of rational beliefs and self-talk is usually cool or warm in emotional tone rather than hot or volatile.

---

* Beliefs, self-talk statements, and automatic thoughts which are irrational and self-defeating can be called "cognitive distortions" or "mistaken ideas" (Beck, 1995: Burns, 1999). I prefer the terms "irrational beliefs and self-talk statements" used in rational emotive behavior therapy (Ellis, 1994).

Beliefs and self-talk statements include:
Irrational beliefs and self-talk statements
Rational beliefs and self-talk statements

Let's look at examples of irrational beliefs and self-talk. After a frustrating experience, you might say to yourself, *"That should not have happened; it was awful and I couldn't stand it!"* Or you might say, *"She has no right to treat me so unfairly, and since she is, that makes me feel worthless, like scum."* Irrational beliefs intensify our emotional upsetness and lead to increased anxiety, anger, and depression as well as maladaptive behavior. Our irrational beliefs sap our mental energy and hinder us from finding creative solutions to our problems.

What are examples of using *rational* beliefs and self-talk? A person might say, *"I wish that bad situation hadn't happened; but it did happen, and I can stand it."* Or in a second example, someone might say, *"She is treating me unfairly and I dislike being treated that way. But, being treated shabbily doesn't make me worthless or less valuable as a person."*

We are responsible for the language we use when talking with ourselves and others. Our self-talk can help us see our problems clearly. Or our self-talk can obscure and delay finding solutions to problems, and intensify our unhealthy, unpleasant emotions.

THE ONE THING PSYCHOLOGISTS CAN COUNT ON
IS THAT THEIR CLIENTS WILL TALK TO THEMSELVES;
AND NOT INFREQUENTLY,
WHETHER RELEVANT OR IRRELEVANT,
THE THINGS PEOPLE SAY TO THEMSELVES
DETERMINE THE REST OF THE THINGS THEY DO.*

* I. E. Farber

The self-talk of generally contented and successful people contains many rational beliefs and statements, even when they experience unpleasant, stressful situations. As mentioned, rational beliefs contain cool or warm language rather than emotionally charged, hot language.

We have looked at A's and B's. Now, let's look at C's. *C's (consequences) are emotions and behaviors that result from our beliefs and self-talk statements.* Emotions and behaviors are consequences of our beliefs and self-talk.

Crooked Thinking
"Common-Sense" View Of Emotions
(Erroneously believing A causes C)
Also called A—C View Of Our Emotions

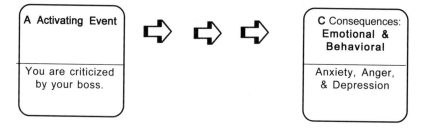

A Activating Event	C Consequences: Emotional & Behavioral
You are criticized by your boss.	Anxiety, Anger, & Depression

Straight Thinking
Accurate View Of Emotions
(Correctly believing A activates B but B causes C)
Also called A—B—C View Of Our Emotions

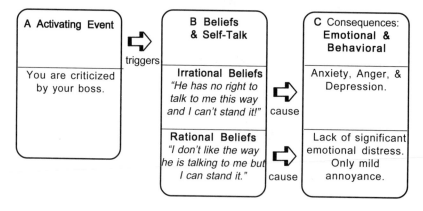

A Activating Event		B Beliefs & Self-Talk		C Consequences: Emotional & Behavioral
You are criticized by your boss.	triggers	**Irrational Beliefs** *"He has no right to talk to me this way and I can't stand it!"*	cause	Anxiety, Anger, & Depression.
		Rational Beliefs *"I don't like the way he is talking to me but I can stand it."*	cause	Lack of significant emotional distress. Only mild annoyance.

Emotional consequences include anxiety, anger, and depression, and other unpleasant emotions. But emotional consequences also can include positive emotions such as happiness and contentment.

Behavioral consequences can be positive and self-helping. Or our behaviors can be negative, self-harming, self-downing, and maladaptive. Verbally exploding or getting back at a supervisor or co-worker, after feeling frustrated, can be a self-destructive behavioral consequence of your frustration.

Which characterizes you, crooked thinking or straight thinking? *Straight thinking is acknowledging that events and situations influence us, but that our rational and irrational beliefs and self-talk statements influence us much more.* Straight thinking is recognizing that our B's (beliefs and self-talk statements) mainly cause our C's (consequences: emotional & behavioral). Straight thinking is A—B—C Thinking.

Be a straight thinker rather than a crooked thinker! Straight thinkers have more fun in life and less distress!

Straight Thinking vs Crooked Thinking

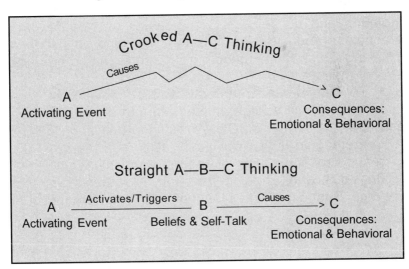

Note that B's (Beliefs & Self-Talk) are absent in Crooked A–C Thinking.

Crooked thinking, also called A—C Thinking, is believing that we have little or no ability to influence our feelings and that events and situations directly cause our emotions and behavior. Many unhappy people, awash in their emotions of anxiety, anger, and depression, despairingly claim that unpleasant events cause their feelings, and that they are powerless to soothe their feelings and improve events in their lives. They have lost touch with their irrational beliefs and self-talk statements since these beliefs and statements have become so rapid, automatic, and habitual. As an early Greek philosopher said, "*People are disturbed not by things, but by the views which they take of them.*" As well as feeling miserable, people who think crookedly are much less able to achieve their short and long term goals.

People are born with potential for engaging in both crooked and straight thinking and behaving in both self-defeating and self-helping ways (Ellis, 1994). Some people live continuously in self-imposed misery, endlessly repeating the same mistakes in day-to-day living. *However, they can learn to live more successfully and happily if they first straighten out their irrational beliefs and self-talk.*

Effectively learning SOS involves practicing its methods and concepts. Get a pencil and paper, and practice reproducing the "Straight Thinking vs Crooked Thinking" illustration. Later, set SOS aside and reproduce it from memory.

To live more contentedly and effectively requires knowledge of the straight thinking taught in REBT, and a self-analysis of your ABC's. Practicing and applying the ABC method in your own life is also necessary. Take increased responsibility for creating and managing your feelings of anxiety, anger, depression, and other unpleasant feelings. Spend less time blaming people and events out of your control.

CROOKED THINKING
IS STINKING THINKING!

Three Major Musts –
Harmful Irrational Beliefs

As we go through life, we have thousands of thoughts each day. Some of these thoughts get us into emotional difficulties. Which ones do we need to change? Albert Ellis, the founder of rational emotive behavior therapy, has identified the core irrational beliefs leading to emotional difficulties. Let's look at the most common irrational beliefs and self-talk statements which cause us so much misery.

Three Major _Musts_: Irrational Self-Talk

1. *I MUST ...!*

2. *You (he or she) MUST ...!*

3. *The world and the conditions under which I live MUST ...!*

We largely cause and intensify our anxiety, depression, and anger by believing specific irrational beliefs, and repeating particular self-talk statements to ourselves. These self-talk statements *demand* that things be different. We place these demands on ourselves, on others, or on the world and conditions under which we live.

These irrational beliefs are <u>demands</u> that, *"I, others, or the world must be different; and if I, others, or the world are not different, then that is awful, I can't stand it, and then I will be anxious, angry, or depressed."* Few people are completely aware of their irrational beliefs because these beliefs are partly unconscious.

Best In Sales

Bill, a thirty-five year old successful car salesperson believed, *"I must always be best in sales at the auto dealership, and if I am not, as I absolutely must be, then I can't stand it. And then I will always be second or third rate and that would mean I am worthless. I couldn't stand myself; others wouldn't respect me; and I wouldn't respect myself!"* Bill functioned under so much threat each day that when he arrived at work he was apprehensive, on edge, and easily annoyed. And when he left work he continued feeling the same way. At home he was grumpy, easily irritated, and withdrew from his wife and children. Bill's demand that he absolutely must be the best car salesperson is directed toward himself because he believes the first major must: *"I MUST...!"*

If instead, Bill placed rigid demands on his boss to provide him with a better office or to advertise more, then he would be clinging to the second major must, *"You MUST...!"* The second major must or demand usually leads to feelings of anger at the other person.

If Bill's self-talk rigidly demanded that selling cars be easier, less competitive, and more financially rewarding, he would be adhering to the third major must, *"The world and the conditions under which I live MUST ...!"*

When "shoulds" are used like the three major musts, the shoulds are called "absolute shoulds" and they are likewise harmful to our emotions.* For example, if you are upset with a co-worker and tell yourself, *"He must treat me with a lot of respect and if he doesn't, as he absolutely should, he should be damned!"* The words "ought" and "has to," when used as absolute demands, also serve in the same harmful way as musts and absolute shoulds.

---

* Technical Talk about kinds of shoulds and musts: *Absolute demanding shoulds, musts, should nots, oughts, ought nots,* and *have to's* are all harmful self-talk statements. When you use these demanding, absolute shoulds and musts you are demanding that you, others, or the world be different. There are five kinds of shoulds which are <u>not</u> used in an absolute, demanding way and these are harmless. These are shoulds of preference, recommendation shoulds, ideal shoulds, empirical-factual shoulds, and conditional-tentative shoulds.

People have an inherent tendency to escalate their wishes and preferences into musts, absolute shoulds, and demands which they place on themselves, others, and the world. These people then become miserable when others and the world don't comply with their rigid demands to change. It's irrational to believe the world will change to fit your needs and demands. Modify your self-talk and avoid shoulding or musting on yourself.

Three Absolute Shoulds: **Irrational Self-Talk**

1.   *I absolutely Should ...!*

2.   *You (he or she) absolutely Should ...!*

3.   **The world and the conditions under which I live absolutely Should ...!**

Loretta, a bright student, almost obtained straight "A's" in her college classes. On one particular exam in my class she received a "B." The next day when we happened to meet in the hallway her eyes flashed, she angrily walked up to me, burst into tears, and then abruptly walked off. Even though she hadn't said any words, she clearly communicated to me her upset feelings. Later she told me that her self-talk was, *"You have been unfair and you musn't have given me a "B."* Loretta was adhering to the second major must.

For the next exam she worked harder and earned an "A." We were both relieved that she earned that "A!"

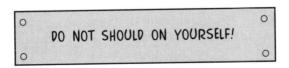
DO NOT SHOULD ON YOURSELF!

Only _preferring_ or _wishing_ that we or others be different while working toward improvement and change is healthy. When we refuse to live with and accept the world as it is, and instead place absolute, rigid demands on ourselves and the world, we suffer emotional problems.

For practice, set SOS aside, get a pencil and paper, and list the "Three Musts or Shoulds" from memory.

The Three Major Musts:
Carrying Excess Emotional Baggage

"I sure have a lot of problems. Most of the time I feel anxious and tense, angry and *§æ!±»!, and depressed a lot. My counselor says I am causing myself to get upset by my self-talk. But I don't want to believe that..."

Believing the *Three Major Musts* and using them in your self-talk is a primary cause of emotional distress. These three basic musts are: "*I MUST..., You MUST...,* and *the world and the conditions under which I live MUST...*" Practice giving up these irrational beliefs. Traveling through life is difficult, even without a lot of excess emotional baggage.

Blaming or making rigid demands on others, the world, and one's self is the core of most emotional problems. Also, we waste a lot of time waiting for the world to meet our demands. *We have to deal with the world as it is, not as we wish it were.*

Five Hot Connecting Links: Connecting Our Major Musts To Our Emotions

1. **Condemnation & Damnation.***
   Wishing punishment and ruin on yourself or others results in anger directed toward yourself or others. *"You *§æ!±»! louse!"* and *"You SOB!"* are examples.

2. **I-can't-stand-it-itis**.
   I can't stand any discomfort, anxiety, anger, or depression. I can't survive or be happy at all if I have to endure these feelings. I absolutely refuse to accept feeling uncomfortable. This irrational self-talk causes LFT – Low Frustration Tolerance.

3. **Awfulizing**.
   This situation is more than 100% awful; it is HTA - horrible, terrible, awful. *Horribleizing, terribleizing,* and *catastrophizing* are similar to awfulizing.

4. **I'm Worthless**.
   I'm no good at all. Low Self-Acceptance (LSA), low self-esteem, and depression result from this irrational self-talk and thinking. *"I'm a no good, RP (rotten person)!"* is an example.

5. **Always & Never**.
   He, she, or the situation will always be this way and will never change.

Technical Talk: The five hot connecting links are termed "irrational conclusions" or "derivatives from major musts" in rational emotive behavior therapy (Ellis, 1994).

Five Hot Connecting Links –
Harmful Core Irrational Beliefs

Next, let's look at the five hot connecting links and the role they play in shaping our emotions. When people fail to have their musts, shoulds, and other demands met, they tend to create *hot links*. The five *hot connecting links* are also destructive, irrational beliefs and self-talk statements. *The hot links work in conjunction with our major musts and absolute shoulds, connecting our musts and shoulds to anxiety, anger, and depression.*

Let's see how the *musts and hot links* operate together in our thinking and silent self-talk. Phyllis believes, *"The world must give me what I want, when I want it, and if it doesn't, it's an awful place and I can't stand it!"* She is believing the third major *must* and *hot links* one and two. When she tells herself the third major must (*"The world must give me what I want..."*) she will upset herself. However, when she follows that must with the two hot links, 1 (*"and if it doesn't give me what I want, it's an awful place*) and 2 (*I-can't-stand-it*!"), she upsets herself a great deal more.

We cause ourselves considerable anxiety, anger, and depression when we join our musts and our hot links. The links are called "hot" because they contain volatile, emotional language, causing strong, unhealthy emotions. Let's look closely at commonly used hot links.

1. Condemnation & Damnation Of Self Or Others. *Condemning and damning is wishing punishment and ruin upon yourself, others, or life conditions.* This self-talk, creates increased anger and sometimes violent behavior toward others. Condemning yourself is self-downing and creates depression. Swearing is, of course, condemning and damning! An example is saying to yourself, *"That *§æ!±»! driver ahead of me is *§æ!±»! and ought to be taken out and shot!"*

As mentioned in Chapter One, anger is harmful to one's emotions as well as one's cardiovascular system.

Accept yourself, others, and the world as fallible and complex and avoid giving a single overall rating such as *damnation* (Dryden & DiGiuseppe, 1990) or "*§æ!±»!"

2. I-can't-stand-it-itis This self-talk exclaims: "*I can't stand any discomfort, frustration, anxiety, anger, or depression. I can't survive or be happy at all if I have to endure these unpleasant feelings. I absolutely refuse to accept feeling uncomfortable.*"

It is an exaggeration for people to say that they couldn't stand a particular event, because they did not, in fact, die. Although the event was indeed inconvenient or unpleasant, they survived and continued to live. Sometimes people say they can't stand something when in fact they have put up with it for years. Tonya used to say to herself, *"I'll just die if my professor calls on me."* Although her professor occasionally did call on her, she never did die!

I-can't-stand-it-itis creates LFT – Low Frustration Tolerance. Low Frustration Tolerance creates heightened feelings of frustration. LFT saps our endurance for solving problems and achieving our goals, causing anxiety, anger, and depression. LFT causes us to become irritable with ourself and others. Students with LFT readily become discouraged and give up when their studies become difficult.

3. Awfulizing Saying that something is awful is saying that something is more than 100% bad and, usually dangerous and life threatening. How would you respond

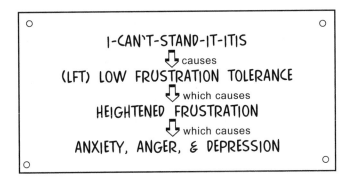

if you were asked, "*What is something that is 100% bad, the worst thing that could happen that you could imagine?*" People usually respond with something like, "*Being with someone I love and we are killed or seriously maimed in an accident.*" If that event is awful (100% bad) how would you rate: losing your job, failing a course, or being overdrawn on your checking account? *Reserve awfulizing for truly awful and dangerous events.*

Unless something is 100% bad, and very few things are, also avoid the hot, self-downing language of *horribleizing, terribleizing,* and *catastrophizing.* When talking with yourself about an upsetting situation, *try substituting the emotionally cool words "bad, inconvenient, hassle, or unpleasant" for hot words such as "horrible, terrible, or awful."*

4. I'm Worthless *I'm worthless means I'm no good at all and have absolutely no use or value.* We are all fallible, and we are all a mixture of good and bad qualities. Realistically, it's not possible for a person to be a 100% RP (rotten person). Using the *I'm Worthless* hot link leads to Low Self Acceptance (LSA), low self-esteem, depression, and shame. When talking with yourself, avoid assigning yourself a negative overall evaluation.

5. Always & Never *Always & never is believing that this person who is behaving badly or this unpleasant situation which is irritating me will <u>always</u> be this way <u>and</u> will <u>never</u> change.* It's not realistic to believe that a situation or person will always be a particular way and will never change. Your emotional reaction to a person or situation certainly can change. Using *always and never* self-talk creates anxiety, anger, and depression.

LEARN WHAT YOU ARE SAYING
WHEN YOU TALK TO YOURSELF.
HEREIN LIES THE KEY TO YOUR EMOTIONS.

CIA, IA – Code For Hot Links

C	Condemnation & Damnation
I	I-can't-stand-it-itis
A	Awfulizing
I	I'm Worthless
A	Always & Never

CIA, IA is a useful way to remember the *Five Hot Links.*

When you are upset about something, listen to what you are telling yourself. Especially, look for your musts and shoulds. And then look for your use of the five hot links. Most self-imposed human misery can be traced to people combining the three musts and hot links. *Whining is when you frequently repeat hot links to yourself and others.*

For practice, set SOS aside, get a pencil and paper and list the names of the *five hot links* from memory. The *five hot links* begin with the letters CIA, IA.

Let's look closer at the connection between the hot links, our musts and shoulds, and our emotions. The diagram, "How Self-Talk Causes Emotions," shows the relationship between *musts, hot links, and emotions.*

Both the *three major musts and the five hot connecting links are irrational beliefs and self-talk statements* which cause and increase the unpleasant, unhealthy emotions of anxiety, anger, and depression.

Preferential shoulds are harmless, unlike absolute shoulds. *Preferential shoulds are preferences, contain cool self-talk language, and don't create hot links* (awfulizing, I can't-stand-it-itis, condemnation & damnation, etc.) *"I should go to the grocery store and get milk since*

HOW SELF-TALK CAUSES EMOTIONS

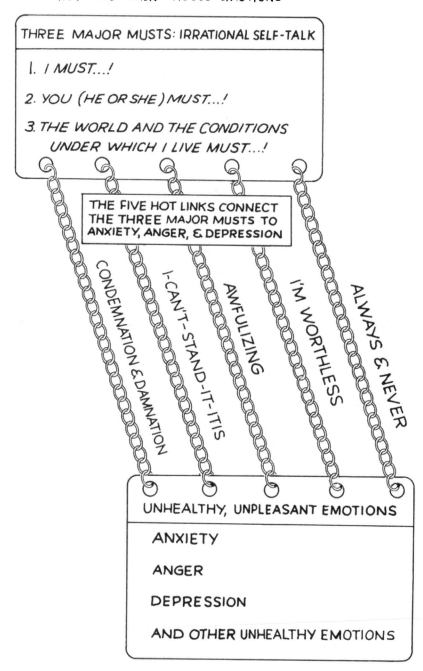

we are running low," is a preferential should statement. *Avoid making absolute should statements when talking with yourself.**

To learn more about the basic nature of people as viewed by rational emotive behavior therapy see Chapter 13, *Information For Counselors.*

TO STRAIGHTEN OUT YOUR EMOTIONS,
FIRST STRAIGHTEN OUT
YOUR BELIEFS AND SELF-TALK

THE ROAD TO REPEATED FAILURES IN LIFE
IS PAVED WITH
IRRATIONAL SELF-TALK & BELIEFS

Main Points To Remember:

- SOS teaches how to use *rational emotive behavior therapy (REBT)* and the *ABC View Of Our Emotions* to help us achieve increased contentment and our goals.

- ABC's explain the source of our emotions. A is the activating event or actual unpleasant event. B is our beliefs and self-talk about the event. C is the consequence in terms of our emotions and behavior.

- Our emotional upsetness is caused mainly by our irrational beliefs, automatic thoughts, and silent self-talk statements rather than by actual events and situations.

---

* Distinguish between your absolute shoulds (unhealthy) and preferential shoulds (healthy). *"I should (absolutely must) get the job for which I am applying and if I don't it will be awful,"* is an absolute should and is unhealthy. *"I should (want to or prefer to) get the job for which I am applying,"* is a preferential should and is healthy.

- Crooked thinkers believe that A's (events and situations) primarily determine our C's (anxiety, anger, depression, and other unpleasant emotions).

- Straight thinkers know that A's (events and situations) influence us, but that our B's (rational beliefs, irrational beliefs, and self-talk statements) influence us much more.

> BE A STRAIGHT THINKER RATHER THAN
> A CROOKED THINKER. STRAIGHT THINKERS
> HAVE MORE FUN IN LIFE AND LESS DISTRESS.

- Insisting on the three basic musts (*I must, you must, and the world and the conditions under which I live must...*) causes us to become anxious, angry, and depressed. *Musts, must nots, absolute shoulds, should nots, oughts,* and *has to* are all harmful self-talk statements when used as <u>absolute</u> <u>demands</u> that you, others, or the world be different.

- The five hot links are also irrational self-talk statements. These include <u>c</u>ondemnation & damnation, <u>I</u>-can't-stand-it-itis, <u>a</u>wfulizing, <u>I</u>'m worthless, and <u>a</u>lways & never. CIA, IA, is a useful code for remembering the five hot links.

> DEAL WITH THE WORLD AS IT IS,
> NOT AS IT "MUST" BE!

> WHEN YOU ARE UPSET,
> LOOK FOR THE MUST, LOOK FOR THE SHOULD!

Chapter 3

Self-Analysis Of Our ABC's

ABC's OF EMOTIONS

WE LEARNED OUR ABC'S

To achieve our goals and increased contentment, it's important that we know the ABC's Of Our Emotions.

A's are activating events, actual events and situations which we encounter, many of which are unpleasant. B's are our beliefs and self-talk statements, what we tell ourselves about these activating events. C's are the consequences that follow and include both emotional and behavioral reactions. These reactions include anxiety, anger, and depression as well as our actions and behaviors.

Our emotions and behaviors mainly result from our beliefs and self-talk statements rather than from actual events in our lives.

We upset ourselves mainly by escalating or advancing our wishes and desires to the level of absolute shoulds, musts, and demands. These demands and musts then become rigid, uncompromising, irrational beliefs which are reinforced by our irrational self-talk statements. The irrational beliefs, when combined with *hot link self-talk statements,* generate intense feelings of anxiety, anger, and depression.

Imagine seventeen year-old Janet, only seven pounds overweight, standing in front of a mirror, saying to herself, " *I can't stand* (a hot link) *being seven pounds overweight. I should* (a major must) *have a perfect body and if I don't, it's awful* (hot link) *and I'm worthless* (another hot link)." How will she feel when going out on a date? Pretty miserable! Her negative evaluation of herself also is likely to be reflected in her manner.

Does Janet absolutely need a 100% perfect body in order to have healthy self-esteem and self-acceptance? No, she doesn't! Since it is not possible to have a truly perfect body, Janet has trapped herself into feeling miserable. She is at high risk for depression, anxiety, and an eating disorder such as anorexia or bulimia.

Wishes, preferences, and desires can't make us miserable. If Janet only says, *"I wish I had a perfect body,"* she won't upset herself. But since Janet is escalating her wish to an *absolute must* followed by *hot links*, she is making herself unhappy.

Janet would be less distressed and better adjusted if she would believe, *"I wish I had a perfect body, and I'll work toward getting an improved body. But if I don't achieve it, it isn't HTA (horrible, terrible, awful), just darn unfortunate, and I-can-stand-it. I just won't like it as much as if I had a perfect body."*

Chapter Six lists and describes the most common irrational beliefs and self-talk statements which cause people to become emotionally disturbed. You might want to browse through some of the irrational beliefs in that chapter.

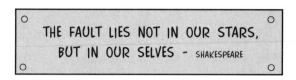

THE FAULT LIES NOT IN OUR STARS,
BUT IN OUR SELVES - SHAKESPEARE

Sources Of
Our Irrational Beliefs And Self-Talk

Our rational and irrational beliefs and self-talk begin in childhood. We learn these beliefs from our parents and family as well as from peers, friends, society-at-large, and especially mass media. Movies, television, magazines, popular songs, and most types of advertising certainly promote many irrational beliefs and expectations.

Elizabeth, a college freshman with a long history of anorexia, looked emaciated. However, her boyfriend told her, *"You look great just as you are now; don't gain a pound!"* He reinforced her irrational beliefs regarding a desirable body, as well as, her unhealthy eating disorder.

In many cases, we don't adopt irrational beliefs from others; our own peculiar thinking creates irrational beliefs and self-talk statements. After we accept irrational beliefs from others or create our own, *we tend to <u>reindoctrinate</u> ourselves continuously with these irrational beliefs and self-talk statements.* We do this by constantly repeating these beliefs to ourselves and acting on them. Once created, irrational beliefs persist in our conscious awareness and in our unconscious unless we actively challenge and modify them.

Carefully focus on the language and words you use when talking with yourself, especially when you feel upset. Your words and language shape your beliefs, as well as, reveal those beliefs.

Become aware of your irrational beliefs and weaken them by studying and practicing the methods and concepts in *SOS Help For Emotions. Weakened irrational beliefs will result in greater contentment and in less anxiety, anger, and depression.*

DEAL WITH THE WORLD AS IT IS,
NOT AS IT "MUST BE"

In order to become more aware of your irrational beliefs and self-talk, practice recognizing examples of straight (rational) and crooked (irrational) thinking. *Straight thinking is recognizing that our beliefs and self-talk statements (our B's) cause our emotions and behaviors (our C's). Crooked thinking is believing that activating events (A's) mainly cause consequences, both emotional and behavioral (C's).* However, as SOS explains, events do not directly cause emotions.

Straight Thinking vs Crooked Thinking

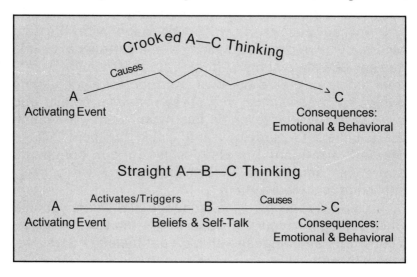

Note that B's (Beliefs & Self-Talk) are absent in Crooked A–C Thinking.

Identify which of the following self-talk statements indicate *irrational, Crooked A—C Thinking* rather than statements which indicate *rational, Straight A—B—C Thinking.* Choose the irrational self-talk statements and compare your choices with the answers listed following the exercise.

Identifying Irrational A—C Thinking:
An Exercise

Identify which of the following are crooked, irrational A—C Self-Talk Statements – believing that events directly cause our emotions.

1. *"She hurt my feelings by what she said."*

2. *"My boss really made me mad, and the more I thought about what he did, the madder I got."*

3. *"I got myself all upset over that clerk's behavior."*

4. *"It made me depressed all day after he told me about that terrible experience he had."*

5. *"I really put myself in a bad mood yesterday after encountering my ex-wife at the mall."*

6. *"Getting locked out of my car this morning made me feel like an idiot!"*

People think mostly in words, phrases, and sentences (Ellis, 1994, p. 35). We positively or negatively evaluate ourselves, others, and our world by our thoughts and silent self-talk statements. Our thinking then determines our emotions and behavior.

Beware of the language that you use when talking with yourself! Avoid irrational A—C thinking and language (believing that activating events cause our emotions). Use A—B—C language (believing that our beliefs cause our emotions) in order to take responsibility for your emotions.

"Charlie's ABC Analysis Of Anger," illustrates the cause of our emotions. We will study D dispute later.

Self-talk statements which reflect irrational A—C Thinking – blaming others or situations for causing us to have an upset mood are sentences 1, 2, 4 & 6. Statements which suggest rational A—B—C Thinking – taking responsibility for our own negative feelings are 3 & 5.

Charlie's ABC Analysis Of Anger

A Activating Event

"He said my nose is too big!"

B Beliefs & Self-Talk

"He has no right to talk to me that way. He must not, he should not have insulted me. He's a *§æ!±»! fool! What kind of *§æ!±»! person would say such a thing! I-can't-stand him saying that!"

Causes

C Consequences:
Emotional & Behavioral Consequences

"I am mad! I am angry! I feel like giving that *§æ!±»! a fat nose! Even if he is the boss, I'm going to tell him off and demand an apology!"

D Dispute

"Wait a minute. I'm making myself mad. He doesn't control my anger; I do. I'm annoyed but I don't have to get angry. I'd prefer that he wouldn't talk to me that way. But I'm responsible for my own anger."

"Charlie's ABC Analysis Of Anger" illustrates the cause of emotions. Let's consider Charlie's ABC's.

<u>A Activating event</u> Apparently the boss said that Charlie's nose is too big.

<u>B Beliefs & Self-Talk</u> Charlie's beliefs and self-talk contain an absolute must, *"He must not..."* Remember from Chapter Two, there are three major musts: I must, you (he or she) must, and the world and the conditions under which I live must... Charlie is stating the second major must, "He must..."
What about hot connecting links? Which hot links is Charlie stating? *Damnation & condemnation* and *I-can't-stand-it-itis* are the two hot links evident in his self-talk.

<u>C Consequences: Emotional & Behavioral</u> What are Charlie's emotions? He is angry! What about his behaviors? Charlie is thinking about telling his boss off and demanding an apology, actions which are self-defeating. He is fantasizing about punching his boss, an action which is not in his best interest!

<u>D Dispute</u> Charlie is disputing his crooked (irrational) thinking. He is realizing that his self-talk is making him angry. You will learn more about D Dispute in Chapter Four.

The "A—B—C Self-Analysis Form" is intended to help us to analyze our irrational beliefs and self-talk. Let's look at "Charlie's A—B—C Self-Analysis Form." This form can help him to understand his emotions and reaction to the unpleasant encounter with his boss. Most importantly, this form will help him to identify his irrational beliefs and self-talk which are responsible for his upset emotions.
You will find this form valuable in understanding your emotions. *When you get upset, analyze your ABC's.* This will help you to manage excessive anxiety, anger, and depression.

Charlie's A—B—C Self-Analysis Form

Date: *5-21-*

A <u>Activating</u> <u>Event</u> (Unpleasant event or situation; can be anticipated events):

My boss said that my nose is too big!

B <u>Beliefs</u> And Self-Talk Statements (Your irrational beliefs and self-talk statements; especially your musts, absolute shoulds, and five hot links):

"He has no right to talk to me that way."
"He must not, he should not have insulted me."
"He's a *§æ!±»! fool!"
"I can't stand him saying that!"

C <u>Consequences:</u> **Emotional & Behavioral** (Your unpleasant emotion and maladaptive behavior):
Emotions:
I feel mad and angry.

Behavior (or contemplated behavior):
I might punch him.
I might tell him off and demand an apology.

> SELF-AWARENESS
> AND AWARENESS OF OUR SELF-TALK
> ARE MUCH THE SAME.

Copy your own "A—B—C Self-Analysis Form." When upset, complete this form to analyze and modify your emotions.

A—B—C Self-Analysis Form

Date: _____

A **Activating Event** (Unpleasant event or situation; can be anticipated events):

B **Beliefs** **And Self-Talk Statements** (Your irrational beliefs and self-talk statements; especially your musts, absolute shoulds, and five hot links):

C **Consequences:** **Emotional & Behavioral** (Your unpleasant emotion and maladaptive behavior):

Emotions:

Behavior (or contemplated behavior):

The following are steps for doing an ABC Self-Analysis.

First, enter what you think is your A activating event.

Second, write in your C consequences: emotions and behaviors.

Third, listen closely to your B beliefs and self-talk-statements. Then write in your suspected irrational beliefs and self-talk statements. Especially look for your use of the three major musts and shoulds and your use of the five hot connecting links (I-can't-stand-it-itis, etc.). *Detecting your B Beliefs and Self-Talk Statements is the most challenging part of your analysis.*

ABC's OF A TANTRUM

"Waah! I won't do it again! I want down!..."

The A activating event for this child is being placed in time-out.

His B beliefs and self-talk, what he tells himself, include, *"Momma must not have put me in time-out. Since she did put me in time-out, it's awful and I can't-stand-it!"*

His C consequences, both emotional and behavioral, are crying, yelling, pleading, and becoming emotionally upset.*

Two-year-olds have a low frustration tolerance as do some adults. The ABC's for adults are essentially the same as for children. Our B beliefs and self-talk statements primarily cause our emotions rather than unpleasant A activating events. If you are a parent, begin early in helping your child to learn his ABC'c of emotions!

"Faye's ABC Analysis Of Anxiety" also illustrates the cause of emotions and behavior. Let's consider this example. We'll study D dispute in Chapter Five.

---

* The "ABC's Of A Tantrum" illustration is based on a photograph that I took of my two-year-old son Todd after placing him in time-out.

If you are interested in learning how Todd feels about time-out when older, visit the SOS website and listen to an interview with him at age nine. <http://www.sosprograms.com>

Faye's ABC Analysis Of Anxiety

A Activating Event

"Oh! The phone is ringing again! I haven't answered it all day."

Causes

B Beliefs & Self-Talk

"The phone shouldn't be ringing! It's always a problem when someone calls. It might be something I-can't-stand to handle, something awful."

C Consequences:
Emotional & Behavioral Consequences

"I haven't talked on the phone today, and I'm not going to begin now... I'm too upset and tired to talk to anyone anyway. Why does life have to be so difficult? I 'm starting to feel nauseated."

D Dispute

"What law says the phone <u>must not</u> ring? To say it is <u>always</u> a problem when the phone rings is an exaggeration. <u>I</u> <u>can</u> <u>stand</u> talking on the phone, and I can handle even unpleasant situations. I am not going to demand that my life be stress free."

Consider "Faye's A—B—C Self-Analysis Form" in order to become more familiar with using the form.

Faye's A—B—C Self-Analysis Form

Date: 7-10-

A <u>Activating Event</u> (Unpleasant event or situation; can be anticipated events):
The phone rings again.

B <u>Beliefs</u> And Self-Talk Statements (Your irrational beliefs and self-talk statements; especially your musts, absolute shoulds, and five hot links):
"The phone shouldn't be ringing!"
"It's always a problem when someone calls."
"It might be something I can't stand to handle, something awful."
"Why does life have to be so difficult?"

C <u>Consequences:</u> Emotional & Behavioral (Your unpleasant emotion and maladaptive behavior):
Emotions:
I started feeling <u>more</u> tired and upset. I began to feel nauseated. I started feeling <u>more</u> anxious, tense, worried, and overwhelmed.

Behavior (or contemplated behavior):
I didn't answer the phone again this morning.
I've also avoided going out in public and meeting people.

Let's analyze Faye's ABC's.

<u>A Activating Event</u> The phone rings, an event which is not stressful for most people. Also, note that Faye has not answered the phone all day.

    <u>B Beliefs & Self-Talk</u> Faye's self-talk statements contain a major should, *"The phone shouldn't be ringing!"* This statement shows that Faye is using either the second major should (you, he, she, or it must...) or the third major should (the world and the conditions under which I live should...). What about hot connecting links? There are three links: *always & never, I-can't-stand-it-itis,* and *awfulizing.*

    <u>C Consequences: Emotional & Behavioral</u> In terms of emotions, Faye is anxious, tense, worried, and feels overwhelmed by stress. She has physical symptoms of tiredness and nausea. By not answering the phone all day, she might be demonstrating a pattern of marked avoidance behavior – avoiding any people or situations which are even mildly stressful.

    In Part C of the illustration, Faye asks herself, *"Why does life have to be so difficult?"* She is implicitly demanding, *life <u>should</u> be easy.* This demand reflects the third major should, "The world and the conditions under which I live should..."

    <u>D Dispute</u> Faye is learning how to actively detect, dispute, and challenge her irrational beliefs and self-talk. D Dispute will be discussed in the next chapter.

    If Faye doesn't continue challenging her irrational beliefs and improving her emotions and behavior, she could develop an anxiety disorder, such as a *Generalized Anxiety Disorder,* also called GAD. Anxiety disorders are discussed in Chapter Six.

    A Daily Mood Record enables us to keep a log of our mood on a daily basis or throughout a day. It is only an approximate record and doesn't provide a precise measurement or recording. Monitoring our emotions closely is important in later modifying and improving our emotions.

    To better understand our emotions, we need to be more aware of our thoughts, behavior, eating and sleeping patterns, relationships, and body sensations (for example, muscle tightness, onset of headaches). Later chapters provide descriptions of problems and disorders of anxiety, anger, and depression.

Let's look at the record Faye is keeping on her emotions. She is recording the three basic unpleasant emotions: anxiety, anger, and depression. Her distress in terms of anxiety is consistently high. On depression, her distress is moderate. Faye reports that her anger level is only mild.

Faye's Daily Mood Record:
Record Of Anxiety, Anger, And Depression

On a scale from 1 to 10 write in a number corresponding to your average mood for the day. Mild is 1 to 3, moderate is 4 to 5, high is 6 to 8, and severe is 9 to 10.

Date/Time	Anxiety	Anger	Depression	Notes
7-1	7	1	4	
7-2	8	1	3	
7-3	9	1	4	
7-4	8	1	5	
7-5	8	1	4	

Often people are not aware of some emotions. It is possible that as Faye becomes more aware of her emotions, she will also be more aware of her anger.

When your upset feelings become moderate or severe, it's time to begin studying your beliefs and self-talk statements which are largely responsible for those upset feelings. The *A—B—C Self-Analysis Form* is a good place to start in better understanding your beliefs and self-talk.

Photocopy or make your own *Daily Mood Record*. Select feelings of anxiety, anger, depression, or other feelings about which you are concerned and keep a log of them. *By monitoring and becoming more aware of your upset feelings, you can modify them more effectively.*

Daily Mood Record:
Record Of Anxiety, Anger, And Depression

On a scale from 1 to 10 write in a number corresponding to your estimated average mood for the day. Mild is 1 to 3, moderate is 4 to 5, high is 6 to 8, and severe is 9 to 10.

Date/ Time	Anxiety	Anger	Depres- sion	Notes

The following directions describe how to keep a Daily Mood Record.

First, decide which of the basic emotions you are going to log. Pay close attention to those emotions. Record your approximate average mood for the emotions you have decided to track. Do this each day. Enter any notes on the record that might help you to better understand your emotions.

WHEN UPSET, ANALYZE YOUR BELIEFS AND SELF-TALK!

> IN ORDER TO MAKE CHANGES IN THE WORLD,
> DEAL WITH THE WORLD AS IT IS,
> NOT AS IT "MUST" BE.

"THE BIG THREE"
UNPLEASANT FEELINGS PIE

The three major unpleasant feelings are
anxiety, anger, and depression.

> NAMING OUR FEELINGS
> IS ESSENTIAL
> TO UNDERSTANDING THEM

Giving Feelings A Name

NAMES FOR PLEASANT FEELINGS

SOS

contented   happy
accepted, liked   glad
appreciated   good, great
capable, confident   grateful, thankful
successful   pleased
comfortable, relaxed   love, loved
eager   satisfied
cheerful, elated   enjoy, like
hopeful, optimistic   proud
encouraged   respected
relieved   secure, safe

NAMES FOR UNPLEASANT FEELINGS

angry, mad   unhappy, miserable
resentful, want to get even messed over, unfair
irritable, grumpy   unloved, neglected
scared, afraid   discouraged
disappointed, let down   embarrassed
lonely, left out   hurt
without a friend, rejected   tired
worthless, no good   bored
stupid, dumb   confused
upset, tense   frustrated
worried, anxious   inferior
insecure   guilty
jealous   ashamed

Learn to be more aware of your feelings by giving them a name. This list gives labels for common pleasant and unpleasant feelings. For a convenient card to review, photocopy this list, cut inside the lines, fold, and tape. Review this list when you are confused about what you are feeling.

THE BURDEN OF
EXCESS EMOTIONAL BAGGAGE

"I am emotionally <u>worn</u> <u>out</u>! I'm one of those unfortunate people that you hear about. I've burdened myself with lots of irrational self-talk. I'm constantly telling myself the three Major Musts and the five Hot Connecting Links."

While traveling through life, some people carry unnecessarily heavy emotional burdens.

The three *major musts* and the five *hot connecting links* are burdens harmful to our emotional well-being. Read on to learn more about how these irrational beliefs and self-talk statements cause continuing anxiety, anger, or depression.

Knowing our feelings and emotions is one of the five abilities of emotional intelligence. An important part of understanding and managing one's feelings is being able to label or name them. When you are confused about what you are feeling, review the list *"Giving Feelings A Name."*

Undoubtedly, you will be experiencing at least several of these feelings, although they may be at a low level of awareness.

Since our feelings spring from our beliefs and self-talk, it's even more important to be aware of our beliefs and self-talk.

LEARN TO SOOTHE YOUR EMOTIONS

Main Points To Remember:

- Awareness of our feelings and awareness of our self-talk are much the same.

- When our upset feelings become moderate or severe, it's time to begin studying our beliefs and self-talk statements.

- ABC's explain the source of our emotions. A is the activating event or actual event. B is our beliefs and self-talk about the event. C is the consequence in terms of our emotions and behavior.

- Our emotions and behaviors mainly result from our B beliefs and self-talk statements, rather than actual events in our lives.

- The *three basic musts* when <u>combined</u> <u>with</u> the *five hot links* generate intense feelings of anxiety, anger, and depression.

- Complete the *A—B—C Self-Analysis Form.* It's a good place to gain better understanding of our beliefs, self-talk, and emotions.

- Consider keeping a *Daily Mood Record* of your anxiety, anger, depression, or other troublesome emotions.

- When you are confused about what you are feeling, review the list *"Giving Feelings A Name."* Naming your feelings is essential to understanding them.

- Weakened irrational beliefs will result in greater contentment and in less stress, anxiety, anger, and depression.

- Test your understanding of the first three chapters of SOS. Turn to Chapter 12 and complete Part One of the quizzes and exercises.

WE THOUGHT THAT THE WORLD WOULD CHANGE,
TO FIT OUR NEEDS... *

---

* "The Class of '54" song by The Statler Brothers, noting the irrational beliefs and expectations of some graduates

Part Two

MANAGING
OUR
EMOTIONS

Chapter 4

Managing Our Beliefs, Self-Talk, And Emotions

"That sign must be straight! I-can't-stand-it being crooked. I'm going to make it level."

Avoid building your life and basing your actions on the *three major musts and the five hot links.* You will find it difficult, if not impossible, to manage your emotions and life while holding irrational beliefs and using irrational self-talk statements.

Managing our emotions is an important part of emotional intelligence, success, and happiness. Controlling our irrational beliefs and self-talk is essential to managing our emotions.

In this chapter you'll learn various methods to help you to manage your emotions. These include:

- distinguishing between *an emotional problem and a practical problem*

- dealing with *our emotional problem before our practical problem*

- replacing our *unhealthy emotions* with healthy ones

- replacing our *musts and shoulds* with *preferences and wishes*

- using *emotionally cool self-talk language*

- practicing *mental imagery*

- learning *coping self-talk statements*

- practicing *deep breathing and muscle relaxation* and

- realizing that some stress reduction activities *help us to feel better but not get better*

We'll learn how the *ABC View Of Our Emotions and Dispute* enables us to challenge and change our irrational beliefs and self-talk. As discussed earlier, SOS follows the rational emotive method, a valuable approach to self-help (Ellis, 1994).

---

* The quote on the prior page, *"The fault lies not in our stars, but in ourselves"* is from Shakespeare. Our problems are determined by our thoughts and actions rather than by the position of the stars at our birth. Also, we can exercise considerable control over our *future thoughts and actions.*

Deal With Our Emotional Problem
Before Our Practical Problem

Most of the problems we encounter can be divided into practical problems and emotional problems. *Practical problems are difficulties and conflicts with others and the external world.* These include poor grades, running two months behind on the rent, and not having a date for Saturday night. *Emotional problems are unpleasant feelings and emotional distress about our practical problems.* Emotional problems include anxiety, anger, depression, jealousy, excessive guilt, shame, and procrastination.* It's important to deal first with our emotional distress about a practical problem, and then to deal with the practical problem.

A Seizure In Venice

My family and I were walking across San Marco Square after visiting the beautiful San Marco Cathedral in Venice, Italy. Ahead, in our path, was a man thrashing about on the ground. Two men rushed over to him and tried to lift him from the ground.

I said to myself, "*Think calmly. This looks like a grand mal seizure. Don't get excited... Trying to carry someone in the middle of a seizure is dangerous.*"

Although my heart was pounding, I immediately walked up to the men. Feeling more confident, I said, *"Stop!"* in English and German. Unfortunately, I was in Italy where people speak Italian. Since I didn't know the word "no" in Italian, I gestured to put the man down. They placed him back on the ground, and I put my folded jacket under his head for protection. After the seizure ended, two people arrived with a stretcher and carried the unconscious man away.

---

* Technical Talk: Practical problems can be thought of as A activating events. Our resulting emotional problems and upsetness are C consequences. We largely control our emotional consequences by our B beliefs & self-talk.

Before helping this man in distress, I tried to calm myself. Then I did what was best for the man which included preventing others from accidentally harming him.

In this stressful situation, I found that I first had to manage my emotional problem (anxiety) with calming self-talk before I attempted to manage the practical problem (a seizure).

After the man was carried away, I remained concerned about him. However, that afternoon I also continued to enjoy seeing the unique buildings which line the Venetian canals.

The stress and strain which we experience from daily living results from practical problems and especially from our emotional distress triggered by those practical problems. After we soothe and manage our emotional reaction to practical problems, we can more effectively solve those reality-based problems. Put first things first. *To solve practical problems, first manage your emotional reaction to them.*

When you become upset about inevitable difficulties in your life, practice asking yourself which of these problems are practical problems and which are emotional problems such as anxiety, fear, anger, and depression.

Deal First With Our *Emotional Problem* Then With Our *Practical Problem*

Practical Problems The situation	*Emotional* Problems You feel...
1. Your six-year-old daughter back-talks you.	1. angry.
2. A friend ignores you at a party.	2. depressed.
3. A car cuts you off in traffic.	3. angry.
4. An especially competent co-worker is hired.	4. fearful and anxious about your job.
5. The exterminator says your home has termites.	5. depressed and anxious.
6. Your car won't start and you will be late for work.	6. frustration.

Your reaction to your six-year-old daughter's sassing or back-talking you might be anger. However, responding with anger, sarcasm, threats, or harsh punishment is usually ineffective and might actually intensify her bad behavior in the long run. If you use sarcasm, you model verbally aggressive, biting behavior which is the same behavior your daughter demonstrated.

Manage your emotional problem (your anger and its expression) before you manage your practical problem (back-talk from your daughter). *SOS Help For Parents* describes effective methods for managing the practical problems which young children present.*

People who readily become angry usually deny having an emotional problem, believing they only have a practical problem. They believe someone else's behavior or a difficult world has made them angry.

```
TO SOLVE PRACTICAL PROBLEMS,
FIRST MANAGE YOUR EMOTIONAL REACTION TO THEM.
```

Decide On A Goal For Your Emotions

How do you want to feel and act as you encounter disappointments, stressful events, and frustrating people? Think about various practical problems which you encounter and your typical emotional and behavioral reactions to these problems. Write down how you *prefer to feel and act* in response to those problems. *Decide on and set a goal for yourself of ways you would like to feel and act when confronted with difficult, practical problems.*

Choose a positive role model for yourself. Think of a person whom you admire because he or she handles challenges and stressful situations effectively and without

---

* *SOS Help For Parents*, a book for parents of children between the ages of two and twelve, is by Lynn Clark and published by SOS Programs & Parents Press. See the end pages of this book for more information about *SOS Help For Parents*.

becoming unduly anxious, angry, or depressed. Let that person be your model. When faced with a distressing situation, ask yourself how this person might handle the problem without becoming overly distressed. Imitate the person's manner, system of rational beliefs, emotional response, and behavior. Don't let the violent action movie heroes, such as Clint Eastwood or Sylvester Stalone, be your role model; this would cause severe problems for you in the real world!

Over the years, my uncle De, has served as a positive model for me. I have often asked myself, when encountering difficult situations and business decisions, how my uncle might feel and act in the same situation. In many situations, my emotional reaction and behavior have been positively shaped by how I imagine my uncle would respond.

Unfortunately, mass media (for example, TV, movies, recordings) provide us and our youth with negative role models for managing anger, aggression, and frustration. Aggressive, violent behavior is becoming increasingly common in the United States. Our homicide rate is seven times higher than that in England, Europe, Japan, and many other developed countries. We, as well as our youth, are exposed to extensive violence, including sexual violence, in the popular media and entertainment programs. Popular heroes in the media frequently "go off on" others and "solve" problems with aggression and violence. Before you encounter stressful situations, *decide how you want to feel and behave.*

Replace Our Unhealthy Emotions With Healthy Ones

To modify our emotional reaction to practical problems, begin with the *ABC View Of Our Emotions.* Think of practical problems as A's or activating events. Our emotional and behavioral response to these practical problems are C's consequences. As the ABC approach teaches, our B's beliefs and self-talk mainly determine our emotions and behavior. Remember, *we primarily cause our own emotions.*

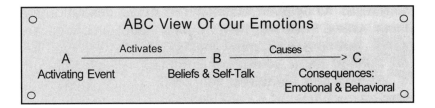

In addition to shaping our emotions with our self-talk, we can replace unhealthy emotions with alternative healthy emotions. When we experience unpleasant events, it's not rational to expect to have pleasant or even neutral emotions. Often, our emotions will be unpleasant.

However, we can influence the *severity* or depth of our emotional distress when faced with bad events. See the illustration, "Replace Unhealthy Emotions With Healthy Ones," which lists unhealthy emotions and the alternative healthy ones.

Replace Unhealthy Emotions
With Healthy Ones

Unpleasant And Unhealthy Emotions	Unpleasant But Healthy Emotions
1. Anxiety & Fear	1. Concern
2. Rage & Anger	2. Annoyance
3. Despair & Depression	3. Sadness
4. Extreme Frustration	4. Disappointment
5. Severe Guilt	5. Remorse
6. Severe Hurt	6. Disappointment
7. Shame	7. Regret
8. Extreme Jealousy	8. Mild Jealousy
9. Humiliation	9. Embarrassment
10. Self-Hate	10. Disappointment with intent to improve

All of the emotions listed in the above illustration are unpleasant. However, <u>healthy</u> unpleasant emotions are less severe and upsetting. Feeling less distress, you will more effectively solve practical problems. Replacing your unhealthy unpleasant emotions with healthy ones is a goal.

Replace Musts And Shoulds With Preferences And Wishes

Don't escalate your preferences and wishes into demands, musts, and absolute shoulds. When you discover that you are musting and shoulding, change your musts and shoulds into wishes, preferences, and desires. Avoid using the five hot links. Musts, absolute shoulds, and hot links are all unhealthy irrational beliefs and self-talk.

Our unfulfilled wishes, desires, and preferences can't make us miserable. However, our absolute demands (musts, must nots, shoulds, and should nots), when connected with the hot links (condemnation & damnation, I-can't-stand-it-itis, awfulizing, I'm worthless, and always & never), can make us miserable.

"People start with a wish and make it into a demand. By disputing loudly, strongly, and repeatedly, they can try to turn it into a wish again (Ellis, 2001)."

"Demands [that is, the three musts] lead to emotional upsetness, preferences lead to emotional stability (Morris in Weinrach, 1996)." *Change your demands and musts into wishes and preferences.*

> ○   ○
>
> UNFULFILLED PREFERENCES, WISHES, AND DESIRES
> CAN'T MAKE US MISERABLE.
> ABSOLUTE DEMANDS, MUSTS, AND SHOULDS
> CAN.
>
> ○   ○

Use Emotionally Cool Language

Use emotionally cool language when talking with yourself and others, especially in situations in which you might become excessively upset. Avoid hot, emotionally charged language because your thoughts and language cause your emotional upsets.*

Imprecise use of language is a cause of distorted thinking (Corey, 1996, p. 329). Our language shapes our thinking; Our thinking shapes our language; Our thinking and language shape our emotions and behavior.

Instead of describing a bad situation as "awful" to yourself, describe it as "inconvenient." The situation will be a little easier to tolerate emotionally.

Imagine a thermometer. Let mercury in the thermometer represent the heat of your emotions. The cause of the heat is your beliefs and your self-talk. Visualize turning down the heat in your language and watching the mercury in the thermometer and the heat in your emotions fall.

A common misconception is that hot, aggressive, "powerful," language that challenges, damns, and condemns others and the world will reduce anger by venting angry feelings. You might momentarily feel pleasure by expressing intense anger. However, you are practicing hot thoughts and actually increasing your total burden of anger. Both expressing anger *and* carrying a load of unexpressed anger cause cardiovascular problems

WE PRIMARILY CAUSE OUR OWN EMOTIONS.

---

*Technical Talk: Therapists call hot, emotionally charged language "hot thoughts" or "hot cognitions" and contrast them with healthy "cool thoughts."

Teenagers sometimes tell a friend "to chill out" when they see that friend start to become upset and angry.

Emotions Thermometer:
Hot Language And Self-Talk Cause Hot Emotions

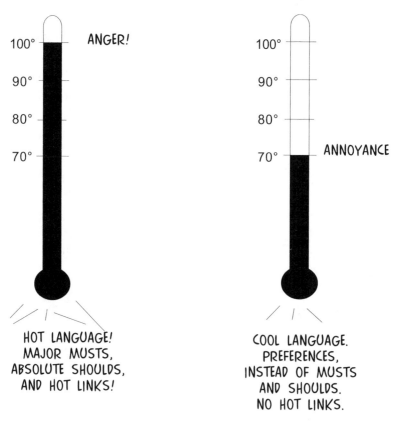

Practice Negative Then Positive Mental Imagery

An Exercise In Mental Imagery

Use negative mental imagery. *Negative mental imagery is visually imagining yourself again experiencing the same bad situation with the same degree (or more) of emotional upset that you experienced the first time.* Hold this negative image and feeling for a minute or so.

Then slowly change this unpleasant image, and feeling into a more pleasant image and feeling. *Use positive mental imagery. Imagine the same bad event or situation, but this time imagine feeling less upset and behaving more rationally.* This is positive mental imagery. Continue to practice positive mental imagery and continue to replace old, unhealthy emotions and behaviors with new, less distressing, healthy emotions and behavior.

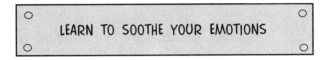

LEARN TO SOOTHE YOUR EMOTIONS

Why use negative mental imagery, as well as, positive mental imagery? Intentionally using both negative and positive imagery helps you to distinguish clearly between these two types of imagery.

Using negative then positive mental imagery is helpful in coping with old unpleasant situations and with future, anticipated stressful situations such as asking for a raise or for a date. However, mental imagery is helpful only if you practice it.

An unhealthy form of negative imagery is repeatedly imagining yourself punishing someone with whom you are angry – someone who has transgressed one of your major musts. This is called the *"Punishing Hero Fantasy."*

Avoid the trap of practicing only negative mental imagery. Unfortunately, some people repeatedly visualize themselves again experiencing old unpleasant situations with the same unhealthy emotions and behavior which they experienced in the original situation. They do this *without* also practicing positive mental imagery. *Practicing only negative mental imagery is harmful and leads to obsessive thoughts, as well as, increased anxiety, anger, or depression.* It's especially important to practice positive mental imagery.

Fired At Age 55 —
And Practicing Only Negative Mental Imagery

Barb, a 55 year-old business executive, lost her job due to corporate downsizing and cost savings. When she arrived at work one Monday she was met by two executives who told her, *"Your job has been eliminated. Clean out your desk and leave."* Barb was caught by surprise, cried, and begged for her job. She was still emotionally distraught when her bosses escorted her to the parking lot and her car.

For months Barb often replayed the upsetting events of that Monday. She repeatedly thought to herself, *"It's unfair what they did to me and the way they fired me. They shouldn't have fired me. I-can't-stand not having my job. And I-can't-stand myself for the disgusting way I acted that day."* Each morning when awakening, the first thing Barb thought of was being fired. Each night before falling asleep, it was the last thing she thought about. Barb was miserable.

By constantly replaying only the bad events, Barb continuously practiced harmful negative imagery. She remained intensely angry at the company and also at herself because of her behavior that day. Barb would not give up her irrational beliefs, hot thoughts, major musts, hot links, and negative mental imagery which were fueling her severe and continuing depression, anger, and misery.

Use Coping Self-Talk Statements

When you feel extremely frustrated or upset, use coping self-talk statements to help manage your emotions.* Such statements replace crooked thinking, irrational self-talk, and unhealthy emotions.

---

* Technical Talk: Coping self-talk statements are closely related to dispute statements which will be discussed in Chapter Five.

The following are examples of coping statements:
"Life is tough."
"Life is tough but I can stand it."
"I don't like this, but I can stand it."
"Life is grim sometimes."
"The world is absurd."
"I don't like it, that's ok, I can stand it anyway." **

When something frustrates me, I personally find the following jingle helpful, *"I don't like it, that's ok, I can stand it anyway."* Repeating this jingle to myself (at least three times) helps me to feel less frustrated and stressed by a bad situation. If you are a parent, teach it to your child and practice together. You will both learn an additional method for managing your emotions.

Develop additional coping statements for yourself to use when you feel anxious, angry, or depressed. *Develop cool language coping statements.*

I DON'T LIKE IT, THAT'S OK,
I CAN STAND IT ANYWAY.

Distraction, Diversion, And Entertainment

Become involved in some pleasurable activity in order to get a break from what is troubling you. However, avoid the harmful diversion traps of overeating, smoking, drinking excessive alcohol, taking "recreational" drugs, and engaging in other activities known to be self-harming.
Distraction and diversion provide helpful, but only temporary, relief. *Diversion and distraction help you to feel better, but not to get better.* For more lasting relief, change your major musts and hot links.

**Jingle is from Nottingham (1994) & Albert Ellis Institute For Rational Emotive Behavior Therapy.

Practice Deep Breathing
And Progressive Muscle Relaxation

Daily, or when tense, anxious, or upset, practice relaxation exercises. Lie down or sit in a comfortable chair.

Deep Breathing Instructions: Close your eyes and empty your mind of thoughts. Take a long, deep breath and visualize the fresh air entering your nose and filling your lungs. Focus on your breathing and the sound of the air. With each breath, think the word "calm" or "relaxed."
Focus on the new air, relax, and hold this breath for as long as it is comfortable to do so. As you slowly exhale, continue to relax and focus only on your breathing and the air leaving your body.
Continue this deep breathing exercise with another long, deep breath, etc. It is helpful to stay with the exercise for at least ten minutes.

Progressive Muscle Relaxation Instructions: You will progressively tense and relax various muscle groups while you mentally relax. Close your eyes and empty your mind of thoughts.
• Make a tight fist with each hand; hold your fists tightly closed for ten seconds; and focus on the muscle tension. Relax your fists; focus on your fists feeling warm and heavy now that they are relaxed. Silently say, "My fists are calm and relaxed."
• Make your lower and upper arms, as well as your fists, tense for ten seconds. Focus on these muscle sensations. Relax these muscles and focus on their feeling warm and heavy and relaxed.
• Tense your shoulders, neck, face and jaw, as well as, your arms and fists. Follow the above instructions.
• Tense your chest, stomach, back, and above muscle groups. Carry through with the instructions listed above.
• Progressively add additional muscle groups and continue with the same instructions.

Relaxation exercises help you distinguish clearly between tense states and relaxed states. You will notice temporary <u>physical</u> changes and temporary changes in your <u>thinking</u> and <u>feeling</u>. Most people welcome the changes and relaxation brought by progressive muscle relaxation and deep breathing exercises.

Caution: Some people who are troubled with anxiety and panic might initially experience these emotions when practicing relaxation techniques. Because of their automatic self-talk statements, they might interpret their physical or mental changes as catastrophic events. More will be said about *catastrophic misinterpretation of physical sensations* in Chapter Seven, Managing Anxiety.

Relaxation exercises are presented in various self-help programs, books, and tapes. Several weeks of practice are usually necessary before you start benefiting from relaxation exercises. Give yourself time to benefit.

As with distraction and diversion, relaxation exercises provide helpful though brief relief from unpleasant emotions. For lasting help, use the ABC View Of Our Emotions to understand and improve your emotions.

Physical exercise can also help relieve emotional stress and benefit your health as well.

Methods For Achieving Rational Thinking And Successful Living: A Summary

The following is a summary of various methods and techniques for managing your emotions and achieving rational thinking. These methods are discussed throughout SOS and include the following:

- **Acknowledge that beliefs and self-talk mainly cause our emotions,** rather than actual events or practical problems.

- **Use the *ABC View Of Our Emotions* for understanding and improving your emotions.**

- **Deal first with the emotional problem** (your emotional reaction to a practical problem) before attempting to deal with the practical problem.

- **Decide on a goal for your emotions and actions**. Write down how you want to feel and act when you are confronted with stressful or frustrating situations. Choose a positive role model for yourself.

- **Replace unhealthy emotions with healthy ones**. Replace fear with concern.

- **Replace the *three major musts and absolute shoulds* with preferences and wishes**.

- **Drop any of the *five hot links*** (awfulizing, I-can't-stand-it-itis, damnation & condemnation, I'm worthless, always & never) that you are using.

- **Use emotionally cool language when talking with yourself** and others. Let the mercury in a thermometer represent the heat of your emotions, and avoid using hot, emotionally charged language.

- **Keep a Daily Mood Record to better understand your emotions**. Recognize that feelings of anxiety and depression almost always accompany feelings of anger.

- **First practice negative mental imagery, and then practice positive mental imagery**. However, practicing *only* negative mental imagery is harmful and will intensify unhealthy emotions.

- **Use coping self-talk statements** such as, *"I don't like it, that's ok, I can stand it anyway."*

- **Use distraction, diversion, and entertainment** by temporarily becoming involved in some pleasurable activity.

• **Practice deep breathing and progressive muscle relaxation when upset.**

The following are major methods for achieving rational thinking and successful living. These methods have been introduced in this chapter and will be fully described in the following chapter.

• **Detect and identify your irrational beliefs and self-talk** which are mainly responsible for your anxiety, anger, or depression.

• **Dispute and uproot your irrational beliefs and self-talk** which mainly cause your anxiety, anger, or depression. The next section introduces D dispute, a useful method for managing your irrational beliefs and self-talk.

Detect, Dispute, And Uproot
Your Irrational Beliefs
And Self-Talk

Detect means to identify those irrational beliefs and self-talk which are causing you to feel upset. However, it's not enough just to detect irrational beliefs. You also will need to change these beliefs. *Dispute provides you with an effective tool for challenging, weakening, and uprooting particular irrational beliefs and self-talk causing emotional distress. D dispute is debating and disputing with yourself the truth and usefulness of your old irrational beliefs and self-talk.* Disproved irrational beliefs and self-talk will lose their control over your emotions.

Successful *D dispute* of your irrational beliefs helps you build new rational beliefs which lead to new *E's new effects (that is, new emotions and behavior).*

Dispute And ABC View Of Our Emotions

Activating Event	Beliefs & Self-Talk	Consequences: Emotional & Behavioral	Dispute Irrational Beliefs	Effects Of Dispute: New Emotions & Behavior
A —Activates→ B	—Causes—> C		D —Leads to—> E	
	Rational or Irrational Musts Shoulds Hot Links 11 Beliefs	Contentment or Anxiety Anger Depression Procrastination & Irrational Behavior		More Contentment & Reduced Anxiety Reduced Anger Reduced Depression Reduced Procrastination & Coping & Rational Self-Helping Behavior

Some illustrations, such as this one, are repeated since they are especially important. The 11 irrational beliefs will be discussed in Chapter Six.

For an example of Detect and Dispute, consider the illustration, "Road Rage And ABC Analysis Of Anger." People often anger themselves when driving, especially when they are in a hurry.

Our angry driver is learning to dispute her anger. At D she disputes those irrational beliefs causing her anger. She says, *"Wait a minute! I need to remember my ABC's. It's not the situation that upsets me, but what I believe and tell myself about the situation. The car ahead is driving near the speed limit and isn't violating any laws. So I am running late; I can deal with it. Going slower than I prefer isn't awful, and I-can-stand-it. Analyzing my self-talk can help me to manage my emotions."*

We fallible humans have considerable power to upset ourselves and even to bring about emotional and mental disorders. We do this by adhering to irrational beliefs, especially the three basic musts and five hot links.

Road Rage And ABC Analysis Of Anger

A Activating Event

"That car ahead of me is driving too slow. I'm in a hurry!"

Causes

B Beliefs & Self-Talk

"He should go faster! I-can't-stand going this speed, it's awful! What a *§æ!±»! fool he is to frustrate me like this! He should be run off the road!"

C Consequences:
Emotional & Behavioral Consequences

"I am really angry! Anyone would get angry at such a *§æ!±»! driver. I'm starting to get an upset stomach and another headache. And it's all his fault!"

D Dispute

"Wait a minute! I need to remember my ABC's. It's not the situation that upsets me, but what I believe and tell myself about the situation. So I am running late; I can deal with it. Analyzing my self-talk can help me manage my emotions."

After you have initially detected the irrational beliefs and self-talk causing your anxiety, anger, or depression, then go to dispute, the fourth step for managing your emotions.

Repeatedly use dispute to debate, challenge, and weaken those irrational beliefs and self-talk statements which are causing you distress. When you repeatedly and successfully use D dispute, you will experience E effects – new, more positive emotions and behavior. *Successful disputing leads to healthier emotions.*

<u>D</u>ispute Leads To Positive <u>E</u>ffects: New Emotions And Behavior

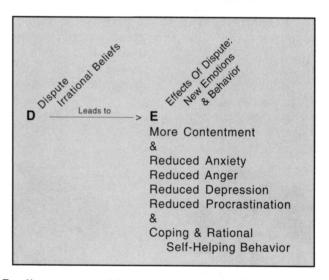

D dispute enables us to take responsibility for managing our anxiety, anger, and depression rather than letting unpleasant situations and other people manage our emotions.

This chapter introduced the methods of *Detect and Dispute.* The next chapter describes and teaches specific methods for detecting, disputing, and uprooting those irrational beliefs which are causing you distress. *Successfully disputing our irrational beliefs and self-talk requires determination and practice.*

Main Points To Remember:

- We largely, but not entirely, cause our own emotions.

- Knowing our irrational beliefs and self-talk is essential to managing our emotions and behavior.

- Set a goal for yourself of ways you would like to feel and act when confronted with difficult people and situations.

- Avoid building your life and basing your actions on the *three major musts and the five hot links*.

- Replace your demands that things *must (three major musts)* go your way, with preferences and wishes that things go your way.

- To solve practical problems, first manage your emotional reaction to them.

- Detect and dispute your irrational beliefs and self-talk which mainly cause your anxiety, anger, or depression.

> I NEVER NEED WHAT I WANT.
> I ONLY PREFER IT.

> I DON'T LIKE IT, THAT'S OK,
> I CAN STAND IT ANYWAY!

Chapter 5

Uprooting Our Irrational Beliefs And Self-Talk

UPROOTING IRRATIONAL BELIEFS

It's not enough to merely identify your irrational beliefs. You'll also need to persistently and forcefully dispute, uproot, and remove them.

Successfully disputing and uprooting our irrational beliefs and self-talk is essential to managing our emotions. This chapter teaches specific knowledge, skills, and methods for detecting and disputing irrational beliefs, enabling us to achieve increased happiness and success. You'll learn:

• how to *detect and identify* irrational beliefs

- *four strategies for disputing and uprooting* irrational beliefs and self-talk

- positive *effects of disputing* (for example, increased contentment and success in achieving your goals)

- how to use the *ABCDE Self-Analysis And Improvement Form* to identify and uproot your irrational beliefs

- how to improve *low frustration tolerance*, a core cause of emotional and relationship distress and repeated failure to achieve goals.

- the difference between *rational thinking and positive thinking*

Musts And Shoulds Defeat Austin

Austin, a fourth semester college student with a history of poor grades, desperately wanted a college degree, but had an irrational plan for achieving one.

While clerking at a convenience food store from midnight to 8:00 am, Austin was carrying a full load of classes. He planned to study at the convenience store, didn't have time to sleep, and was unable to attend many of his classes. Austin was exhausted!

"I <u>must</u> work full time because I need the money, and I <u>should</u> carry a full load of classes because I <u>have to</u> graduate in four years. I'm already behind in my college grades and credits," he explained. "I <u>have to</u> show my parents how hard I am working."

Austin couldn't be persuaded to modify his plans and at the end of the semester, he again received mostly "D's". Austin's <u>musts</u>, <u>shoulds</u>, <u>have to's</u>, and irrational plans now contributed to four semesters of failing grades. Irrational beliefs and self-talk are major causes of emotional distress and failure to reach goals.

Detect your irrational beliefs and self-talk and then dispute them. See D in the diagram, *Dispute And ABC View Of Our Emotions.* Practice talking back to your irrational beliefs and self-talk. What do you say? Read on!

Dispute And ABC View Of Our Emotions

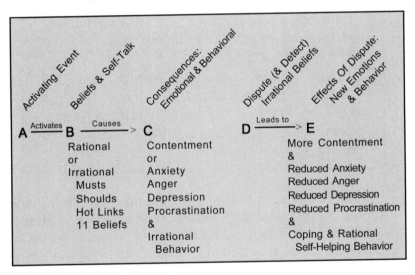

Detect
Irrational Beliefs And Self-Talk

What's the difference between rational and irrational beliefs? Generally, *rational beliefs and self-talk are self-helping and irrational beliefs and self-talk are self-defeating* (Corey, 1996; Nottingham, 1994). "Rational, in Rational Emotive Behavior Therapy, means effectively self-helping" (Ellis, 1994, p. 25).

Rational Beliefs And Self-Talk Are:

- **Logical** – reasonable, sensible, and logical
- **Reality-Based** – based on actual evidence and observation
- **Useful** – helpful, practical, and useful in attaining my goals
  and
- **Enhancing** to self, others, and relationships
- **Helpful** for emotions; reducing anxiety, anger, and depression
- **Based on preferences and wishes** rather than on the *three major musts and absolute shoulds*
- **Lacking the *five hot links*** (condemnation & damnation, I-can't-stand-it-itis, awfulizing, I'm worthless, always & never)

How do you go about detecting and identifying irrational beliefs and self-talk? The best time to detect your irrational self-talk is when you feel anxious, angry, or depressed about a problem. When you're upset about someone or a situation, apply the *ABC View Of Our Emotions* to the problem or situation that you are experiencing. *Detect your irrational beliefs and self-talk when you are upset.*

Begin with the *ABCDE Self-Analysis And Improvement Form* presented later in this chapter. Complete the steps in the order of A, C, and B so that you can identify the self-talk that is upsetting you. First, determine what you think is the activating event (A). Remember, an activating event can be an actual event or your daydreaming about that unpleasant event.

Second, write in the unpleasant emotions that you are experiencing and any self-defeating behaviors including what you do or say to others (C). Unpleasant emotional consequences include anxiety, anger, or depression. Unpleasant behavioral consequences can include overeating, abusing drugs, exploding at work or home, and other self-defeating behavior.

Third, listen closely to your silent self-talk statements (B). On the form, write in your suspected irrational beliefs and self-talk statements. Usually, your irrational beliefs will be absolute demands that you are placing on yourself, others, or the world. Your irrational beliefs will also be the hot links. You'll need to work hard at detecting your irrational beliefs.

Ask yourself the following questions. They will help you to identify and detect your irrational beliefs and self-talk.

Questions For *Detecting* Irrational Beliefs And Self-Talk

- *What am I saying to myself about <u>myself</u>?*
- *What am I saying to myself about <u>others</u>?*
- *What am I saying to myself about <u>an unpleasant event or situation</u>?**

- *Am I using the three major musts or absolute shoulds? (I must!; he, she or you must!; the world and conditions under which I live must!)*

- *Am I using any of the five hot connecting links? (awfulizing, I-can't-stand-it-itis, damnation & condemnation, I'm worthless, always & never)*

- *What am I telling myself?*

- *What are my thoughts?*

- *What is going through my mind right now?*

- *What does this situation say about my future?*

---

* *"What am I saying to myself ..."* questions were contributed by Dennis Painter in a personal communication.

- *What does this situation say about my education (my marriage, children, job, or status)?*

- *Why am I feeling depressed just thinking about attending that event next week?*

- *What was going through my mind when I experienced that situation?*

- *What were several things going through my mind when I was in that bad situation?*

- *What am I worrying about?*

- *What am I anxious (angry or depressed) about?*

- *What are three things which I am saying to upset myself?*

- *Am I escalating my preferences and wishes into absolute musts or must nots?*

- *Am I demanding that the world be easy?*

- *Am I demanding that the world change to fit my needs or to be an easy place in which to live?*

- *Am I demanding that I get exactly what I want when I want it?*

The *three major musts, absolute shoulds,* and *five hot connecting links* are your most promising leads for detecting your irrational beliefs and self-talk.

```
UNPLEASANT EVENTS AND SITUATIONS
ACTIVATE IRRATIONAL BELIEFS AND SELF-TALK.
```

Disputing And Uprooting
Irrational Beliefs And Self-Talk

After detecting and identifying your irrational beliefs and self-talk, your goal is to forcefully dispute, challenge, uproot and talk-back to them. Replace old irrational beliefs and self-talk with rational beliefs leading to success and to decreased anxiety, anger, or depression.

Dispute Leads To Positive Effects:
New Emotions And Behavior

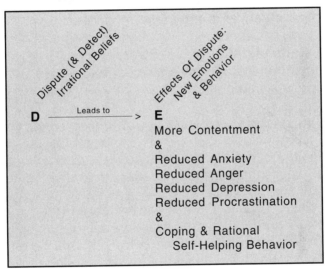

Since past or anticipated unpleasant events and situations activate irrational beliefs and self-talk, the time to dispute these irrational beliefs and self-talk is when you are upset by these unpleasant events.

Therapists teach clients four basic strategies for disputing and challenging irrational beliefs (Beal, Kopec, & DiGiuseppe, 1996). Use these strategies for disputing your irrational beliefs!

Four Strategies For Disputing
And Uprooting Irrational Beliefs And Self-Talk

- **Logical Strategy**:
  Are the beliefs and self-talk reasonable,
  sensible, and logical?

- **Reality-Based Strategy**:
  Are the beliefs and self-talk based on actual
  evidence and observation?*

- **Useful Strategy**:
  Are the beliefs and self-talk helpful, useful,
  and practical in attaining my goals?

- **Rational Alternative Strategy**:
  Are there other more rational alternative
  beliefs and self-talk?

Your goal is to *forcefully and deeply* convince yourself
that your particular irrational beliefs and self-talk statements
causing you to feel upset are *not logical, not reality based,
not useful*, or that there are *rational alternative beliefs and
self-talk*. To convince yourself, you need to engage in
forceful dialogue with yourself and talk back to your irrational
self-talk. Vigorously debate with yourself; argue silently or
aloud; question and challenge your irrational beliefs.

How long does this forceful dispute need to last?
Five to ten minutes is usually not enough time. After you
detect an irrational belief or self-talk statement, ask the
irrational side of you to present its case. Then ask your
rational side to challenge and debate against this irrational
belief. Continue the debate with your irrational and rational
sides taking turns. The more resistive your irrational
belief, the more often you will need to engage in these
dispute sessions. *Continue disputing an irrational belief
until you no longer believe it.*

---

* Technical Talk: Reality-Based Dispute Strategy is also described as empirical
and scientific. Useful Dispute Strategy is described as pragmatic and functional.

Forcefully uproot those irrational beliefs and self-talk statements which cause you to feel anxious, angry, or depressed. Remind yourself that you are making progress by acknowledging that your *beliefs about unpleasant events* are mainly causing your unhealthy emotions.

Frequently challenge the *three major musts* and *five hot connecting links* since they are responsible for most of your emotional distress. Use the following *dispute statements* to uproot your irrational beliefs.

```
WHEN UPSET,
LOOK FOR THE MUST, LOOK FOR THE SHOULD!
```

Dispute Statements And Questions
To Uproot Irrational Beliefs And Self-Talk

• **"Logical" Dispute Questions:** Are my beliefs and self-talk about this situation reasonable, sensible, and logical?

Is that self-talk logical and reasonable?

If those beliefs and self-talk statements were held by someone else, would they seem reasonable to me? Where is it written or documented that these beliefs and statements make sense?

Would a reasonable and logical person hold such a belief?

Is it reasonable to believe that such and such will always be this way and never change?

Is it logical to believe that I or anyone else is a "complete failure" because of a failed relationship?

• **"Reality-Based" Dispute Questions**: Are my beliefs and self-talk about the event based on actual evidence and observation?

Where is evidence supporting the truth of this belief or self-talk statement?

Where is there proof for that belief?

Where is it written that I absolutely must get what I want?

Why must she behave the way I very much want her to behave?

Why should I do such and such; where is there evidence that I absolutely must do such and such?

What makes me so special that my life must be easy or that I must get what I want, when I want it?

Is that problem really "awful" or more than 100% bad? Is it worse than the worst thing I can imagine?

Where is the evidence that I "can't stand" that situation (can't survive or physically go on living in that situation)?

Where is there evidence that I am 100% worthless; that I have no good qualities at all?

I lived without this person before. Is there any reason that I can't live without this person now?

Where is proof or evidence that if I failed in one relationship I will never have a successful relationship?

TALK BACK TO
SELF-DEFEATING, IRRATIONAL SELF-TALK

• **"Useful" Dispute Questions:** Are my beliefs and self-talk about that incident or situation helpful, useful, and practical in attaining my goals?

By believing that idea, does it help my depression (guilt, fear, anxiety, anger)?

Do those self-talk statements help me to perform my job better or enjoy my job more?

Does believing that "life must be easy and if it isn't, I-can't-stand-it," help me to reach my goals?

Where does that kind of thinking get me?

Do those beliefs help or hurt me in obtaining my goals?

Does believing that my wife absolutely must do such and such help my relationship with her?

What is the value of insisting that my boss must behave differently, and if he doesn't, he should be condemned and damned?

Does my continuing anger and resentment over the way I was treated help me?

By believing that idea, does it help me to feel better or function more effectively?

Does believing that my teacher is completely unreasonable and is a bad person help me to study harder or get more out of my classes?

Does damning the driver in front of me help the traffic to move smoother? Does it help my blood pressure?

Where does the belief, "Since I failed in one important relationship, I am a complete failure, worthless, and no good" get me in future relationships?

• **"Rational Alternative" Dispute Questions:** Are there other more rational alternative beliefs and self-talk?

Would preferring or wishing that my in-laws not visit, help me feel less upset than thinking that they absolutely must not visit, and if they do, I-can't-stand-it?

Will believing that I am a person with some faults, rather than a totally worthless person, help me feel less tense at the party next week?

Does being calm at work help me to do a better job than frequently feeling angry?

Would preferring to get what I want be less upsetting than demanding that I absolutely must get what I want?

Would believing that I am a person with both strengths and weaknesses help me to relate better to other people than believing, "I am a complete failure, worthless, and no good?"

```
WHAT AM I SAYING TO MYSELF:
       ABOUT MYSELF?
       ABOUT OTHERS?
ABOUT AN UNPLEASANT SITUATION?
```

Effects Of Dispute:
New Emotions And Behavior

Successfully disputing and uprooting our irrational beliefs and self-talk greatly reduces unpleasant emotions of anxiety, anger, and depression. Rational beliefs lead to healthier emotions, more contentment, better coping, and increased ability to attain goals.

<u>D</u>ispute Leads To Positive <u>E</u>ffects:
New Emotions And Behavior

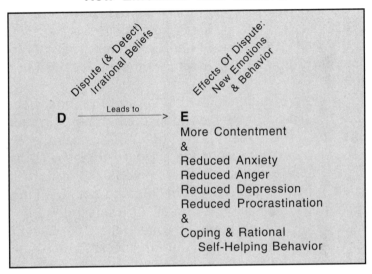

D ——Leads to——> E
More Contentment
&
Reduced Anxiety
Reduced Anger
Reduced Depression
Reduced Procrastination
&
Coping & Rational
Self-Helping Behavior

Rational beliefs and rational self-helping behavior enable us to set and attain our goals. Unburdened of irrational beliefs and unhealthy emotions, you will have more emotional energy to invest in relationships, both personal and those at work or school. Rational beliefs and behavior will increase your feelings of happiness and decrease your level of unhealthy stress. Rational thinking enables you to spend less time struggling with your emotions and more time solving practical problems.

Dispute And ABC View Of Our Emotions: Simplified Illustration

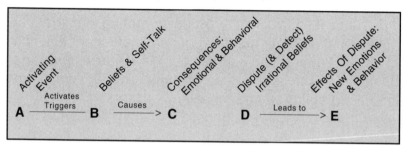

To learn SOS, you'll need to practice its methods. Set SOS aside, get a paper and pencil, and reproduce "Dispute And ABC View Of Our Emotions" from memory. Begin by writing A B C D E with wide spaces between the letters.

As stated earlier, our rational and irrational beliefs begin in childhood. After an individual accepts irrational beliefs from others (such as parents) or creates her own, *she tends to continuously <u>reindoctrinate</u> herself with these irrational beliefs and self-talk statements.* She does this by constantly repeating these beliefs and acting on them. By repeating these beliefs to herself, the roots grow stronger and deeper. Once created, irrational beliefs persist in our conscious awareness and in our unconscious unless they are actively challenged and modified.

You will need to continue detecting, disputing, and uprooting irrational beliefs and self-talk for the rest of your life, in order to live happily and successfully. Particularly, you will need to do this during periods of stress and when you persistently feel anxious, angry, or depressed.

Merely understanding that you are reindoctrinating yourself with irrational beliefs is helpful, but insufficient for emotional change. A weak conviction that your problem beliefs are irrational is not enough. *Deepen your conviction* that your problem beliefs are irrational by actively detecting and disputing them.

Maria Managing Anxiety With ABC's

A Activating Event

"Tomorrow morning, it's my turn to give a five minute speech in class." (Activating events can be anticipated events.)

Causes

B Beliefs & Self-Talk

"I <u>must</u> do well or I'll be humiliated and feel <u>worthless</u>. I-<u>can't</u>-<u>stand</u> everyone watching me so closely. Why does <u>school</u> <u>have to be so hard</u>? I'll <u>never</u> be any good at speaking in front of people."

C Consequences:
Emotional & Behavioral Consequences

"My heart is speeding up; my hands are starting to tremble; and I'm starting to feel sick to my stomach just thinking about giving this impossible speech."

D Dispute

"My demanding that I must do well is causing me to feel really anxious. Although I don't like it, I <u>can</u> stand others evaluating me. If my speech isn't great, I can live with it. Besides, my teacher says I'm improving."

Maria's ABCDE
Self-Analysis And Improvement Form

Date: *8-11-*

A <u>Activating Event</u> (Unpleasant event or situation; can be anticipated events):
Tomorrow morning it's my turn to give a five minute speech in class.

B <u>Beliefs</u> And Self-Talk Statements (Your irrational beliefs and self-talk statements; especially your musts, absolute shoulds, and five hot links):
I <u>must</u> do well or I'll be humiliated and feel <u>worthless</u>. <u>I-can't-stand</u> everyone watching me so closely. Why does school <u>have to be so hard</u>? I'll <u>never</u> be any good at speaking in front of people.

C <u>Consequences:</u> Emotional & Behavioral (Your unpleasant emotion and maladaptive behavior):
Emotions:
My heart is speeding up; my hands are starting to tremble; I'm starting to feel sick to my stomach.

Behavior (or contemplated behavior):
Avoidance of preparing speech.

D <u>Dispute And Debate</u> (Dispute your irrational beliefs and self-talk; especially your musts, absolute shoulds, and five hot links):
My demanding that I must do well is causing me to feel really anxious. Although I don't like it, I can stand others evaluating me. Besides, my teacher says I'm improving.

E <u>Effects</u> (Effects Of Dispute: New emotions and behaviors):
If my speech isn't great, I can live with it. (Maria has reduced anxiety and increased self-acceptance. Reduced anxiety can lead to better performance.)

Analysis Of Maria's ABCDE's.

A Activating Event Maria is thinking about the five minute speech she is giving in class tomorrow.

B Beliefs & Self-Talk Maria's self-talk statements contain a major must, *"I must do well..."* She also asks herself, *"Why does school have to be so hard?"* This question is actually a demand that school be easy. She is requiring that school, the world, and the conditions under which she lives be easy, accepting, nonjudgmental, and noncritical.

What about hot connecting links? Maria is using three links: *I'm worthless, I-can't-stand-it-itis*, and *always & never*.

C Consequences: Emotional & Behavioral Maria's self-talk is causing her to feel highly anxious, tense, worried, threatened, and to doubt her self-worth. She has significant physical symptoms of anxiety including an accelerated heart rate, minor trembling, and nausea.

In addition to feeling highly anxious, she is procrastinating and avoiding work on her speech.

D Dispute Maria is learning how to dispute and uproot her irrational beliefs and self-talk. Instead of continuing to believe, *"I-can't-stand everyone watching me so closely,"* she says, *"Although I don't like it, I can stand others evaluating me."* Instead of believing *"I must do well,"* she says, *"If my speech isn't great, I can live with it."* Instead of believing, *"I'll never be any good at talking in front of people,"* she says, *"And, my teacher says I'm improving."*

Maria is learning that her beliefs and self-talk are mainly causing her anxiety: *"My demanding that I must do well is causing me to feel really anxious."* What Maria believes and tells herself about her speech, can cause greater threat and anxiety than the speech itself.

<u>E Effects Of Dispute: New Emotions And Behavior</u>
As a result of disputing her irrational beliefs, Maria feels less anxious, less threatened, and more in control of her emotions. She said, *"If my speech isn't great, I can live with it."* She is learning to accept herself and to feel less vulnerable to evaluation and criticism by others.

"A little anxiety helps to focus the mind, but too much paralyzes it," according to a Chinese proverb.* By managing her level of anxiety, Maria undoubtedly will think more clearly and give a better speech.

Maria needs to continue challenging her irrational beliefs and managing her emotions, especially anxiety. If she doesn't, she could develop an anxiety disorder such as *Social Phobia (Social Anxiety Disorder).* Anxiety disorders are discussed in Chapter Seven.

When feeling especially anxious, angry, or depressed, complete an "ABCDE Self-Analysis And Improvement Form," as did Maria.

First, enter what you think is your A activating event.

Second, write in your C consequences: emotions and behaviors.

Third, listen closely to your B beliefs and self-talk statements. Then write in your suspected irrational beliefs and self-talk. Especially look for your use of the three major musts and shoulds and your use of the five hot connecting links (I-can't-stand-it-itis, etc.). To remember the five hot links, remember "CIA, IA" described in an earlier chapter. Also review the 11 common irrational beliefs presented in Chapter Six. Detecting your B beliefs and self-talk statements is the most challenging part of your analysis.

Fourth, D dispute and challenge your irrational beliefs and self-talk using the methods described in this chapter.

Lastly, write in your E effects of dispute: new emotions and behavior.

Continue detecting your irrational beliefs and self-talk and uprooting those beliefs and self-talk statements causing you distress. Use the *ABCDE Self-Analysis And Improvement Form* whenever you feel distressed.

---

* Tao He, one of my students from China, told me of this proverb.

ABCDE
Self-Analysis And Improvement Form

Date:

A <u>**Activating Event**</u> (Unpleasant event or situation; can be anticipated events):

B <u>**Beliefs**</u> **And Self-Talk Statements** (Your irrational beliefs and self-talk statements; especially your musts, absolute shoulds, and five hot links):

C <u>**Consequences:**</u> **Emotional & Behavioral** (Your unpleasant emotion and maladaptive behavior):
Emotions:

Behavior (or contemplated behavior):

D <u>**Dispute And Debate**</u> (Dispute your irrational beliefs and self-talk; especially your musts, absolute shoulds, and five hot links):

E <u>**Effects**</u> (Effects Of Dispute: New emotions and behaviors):

Copy this form. Complete the steps in the order of A, C, B, D, and E. When upset, follow the self-help methods in Chapters 4 and 5. As you complete B, look for your musts, shoulds, and hot links. Also, see if you are believing any of the 11 irrational beliefs described in Chapter Six.

Low Frustration Tolerance (LFT)

No low frustration tolerance!

Low tolerance for frustration is caused by the irrational
belief – *"The world must be easy."*

To increase your capacity to bear frustration, repeat
the coping jingle – *"I don't like it, that's ok, I can stand
it anyway. I don't like it, that's ok, I can stand it anyway."*

Let's look at frustration, frustration tolerance, low
frustration tolerance (LFT), and how they relate to emotional
stress.

Frustration "is not getting what you want" (Ellis, audio).
It's having your wishes, efforts, and plans blocked.
*Frustration tolerance is the amount of discomfort you
believe you can tolerate.*

*Low frustration tolerance (LFT) is believing the world
is too hard <u>and</u> telling yourself, "I can't stand its being so
hard."* Frustration, for example, is driving your golf ball
into the rough. *Low frustration tolerance* is driving your
golf ball into the rough <u>and</u> *telling yourself, "I must not get
a poor drive and since I did get a poor drive, these clubs
are awful and I can't-stand-it. I'll never be any good."*

An interesting discussion of LFT is, *Conquering Low Frustration Tolerance* by
Albert Ellis. This audiotape is available from Albert Ellis Institute For Rational
Emotive Behavior Therapy.

Apply the *ABC View Of Our Emotions* to understanding your low frustration tolerance and distress. Driving the ball into the rough is an activating event. Your irrational belief and self-talk is, "*I must not get a poor drive and since I did get a poor drive, these clubs are awful and I can't-stand-it, I'll never be any good.*" Consequences, both emotional and behavioral, include getting angry at your clubs, becoming emotionally upset, and perhaps playing poorly the next few holes because you are upset. Remember, *you primarily cause your own emotions.* Avoid blaming the activating event as the sole cause of your distress.

Whereas, frustration is a normal part of life, LFT is a major cause of distress, unhappiness, procrastination, and poor performance. To reduce your LFT, work on increasing your tolerance or capacity to bear frustration without becoming emotionally upset. Don't expect to get completely rid of frustration because frustrating events will always occur, and a positive effect of frustration is that people usually learn to reduce and improve obnoxious events.

A rational goal is improving our low frustration tolerance (something within us) rather than expecting to get rid of frustration (the outside world blocking our wishes). Do detect and dispute the irrational beliefs and self-talk causing your low frustration tolerance.

Some people erroneously believe they can reduce strong feelings of frustration by venting their anger. Becoming angry and obnoxious when frustrated actually increases the likelihood that you will respond the same way or more intensely in the future. Anger and poor ability to tolerate frustration reduce our problem-solving ability and impair our performance. Becoming angry and obnoxious creates stress in others, often damages important relationships, and may cause others to hold a grudge. Improve your low frustration tolerance, and reduce your distress by adjusting your self-talk. See the illustration, "Raising Your Low Frustration Tolerance."

Raising Your Low Frustration Tolerance

Irrational Beliefs Causing LFT:	Rational Beliefs Helping Your LFT:
It's awful!	*It's inconvenient.*
It's too hard.	*It is hard. It is difficult.*
It shouldn't be so hard.	*It's hard & that's the way it is.*
It shouldn't be this hard.	*There's no evidence it should be easier.*
Nothing should be this hard.	*Why should the world be easy?*
When I fail, the world is unfair and a miserable place to live.	*When I fail, the world is as it is. I will improve next time.*
I can't stand frustration!	*I don't like frustration but I can stand it.*
Difficulties and hassles are horrible, terrible, & awful (HTA).	*Difficulties and hassles are inconvenient and unpleasant.*

GET IN TOUCH WITH YOUR FEELINGS.
AND GET IN TOUCH WITH YOUR SELF-TALK,
BECAUSE IT MAINLY DETERMINES YOUR FEELINGS.

I can't-stand-it-itis self-talk, is a major cause of LFT. If you repeat *"I can't-stand-it"* often enough, you will come to believe it's a scientific fact.   When feeling frustrated, use coping statements such as, *"I don't like it, but I can stand it"* or *"I can put up with things I don't like."* Also, remember the jingle, *"I don't like it, that's ok, I can stand it anyway."*

The major cause of LFT is I-can't-stand-it-itis and the cure is I-can-stand-it.

COPING WITH FRUSTRATION BY RAISING FRUSTRATION TOLERANCE

"I don't like it, that's ok, I can stand it anyway....
I don't like it, that's ok, I can stand it anyway....
I don't like it, that's ok, I can stand it anyway...."

We can't always control frustrating situations, but we can control and manage our distress and emotional reaction to them. This unfortunate man is using coping self-talk to control his frustration.

Unfortunately, some people have a great deal of frustration, that is, not getting what they want. *"The more unlucky you are .... the more you are frustrated (by the economy, politicians, etc.), the more you had better work on your low frustration tolerance"* (Ellis, audio). The more frustration you experience from unfair, unpleasant events and people, the more you can benefit from SOS.

> THE MORE YOU ARE FRUSTRATED,
> BY UNFAIR PEOPLE AND EVENTS,
> THE MORE YOU NEED
> TO IMPROVE YOUR ABILITY TO BEAR FRUSTRATION.
> THIS IS ESPECIALLY TRUE IN TIMES OF CRISIS.

After considerable thought you may decide to take strong or extreme action to correct a bad situation. You can take more effective and measured action by first managing your self-talk, feelings, and capacity to bear frustration.

Positive Thinking

Rational thinking is different from positive thinking. *Positive thinking is confidently expecting a positive outcome to problems or life events, believing that a situation will improve.*

Rational thinking is maintaining a realistic and positive view of events, guarding against our irrational beliefs sabotaging our goals, and effectively helping ourselves adjust to events even if they become unpleasant or adverse. Simply put, positive thinking is believing that events will improve. And rational thinking is helping ourselves to be reasonably well-adjusted even if events don't improve.

Rational Thinking Is More Than Positive Thinking

Positive Thinking	Rational Thinking
1. I will keep my job.	1. I don't think I will lose my job, but if I do I can stand it. And I will try to get another one.
2. My relationship with the wonderful guy I am dating will continue. Things will work out.	2. If my relationship ends with the wonderful guy I am dating, it will be unfortunate, but not awful. I will be able to start another meaningful relationship.
3. My son is going to behave when we go shopping this afternoon, and others will see how well behaved he is.	3. My son will probably behave when we go shopping this afternoon. If he doesn't behave, that doesn't mean that he is a brat or I'm a bad parent.

Sprayed With Mace

One of my college students went to an extreme to find something positive in an unpleasant event. Her mischievous little brother sprayed her in the face with mace. She explained to me, *"I'd been having a lot of trouble with clogged sinuses. Getting sprayed with that mace really cleared out my sinuses. I haven't had trouble with them since!"*

Surviving A Lightning Strike

A woman surviving a lightning strike said that she felt like a lucky person because she was hit by lightning and she survived. A man also surviving a lightning strike explained that he felt like an unlucky person because he was hit in the first place!

How you feel about bad events largely depends on what you believe and tell yourself about the events.

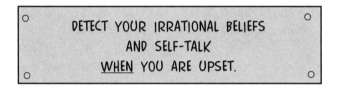

DETECT YOUR IRRATIONAL BELIEFS
AND SELF-TALK
WHEN YOU ARE UPSET.

Which belief system, *Rational Beliefs* or *Irrational Beliefs,* would you prefer that your child or someone you love live by?   Upon which system would you want to depend during the storms in your life?

Rational Beliefs

"I am mainly responsible for my own feelings of happiness and unhappiness as well as for success in reaching my goals. Life is full of beauty and pleasure but sometimes life is bleak and grim."

"I will strive to know the difference between what I can change and what I cannot change. I will work at changing the things I can. When I feel persistently anxious, angry, or depressed I will work at reducing these feelings. I will work at accepting and coming to terms with what I cannot change. Even when the realities of life are bleak and grim, I will do my best to adjust and live with calmness."

Harmful Irrational Beliefs

"Other people and events (including early events in my life) mainly cause my present feelings and behavior. Pleasant events and supportive people cause my happiness and my success in reaching goals."

"When grim events occur, I can't help but feel miserable. I have little ability to control my emotions and behavior. When I feel persistently anxious, angry, or depressed, I blame myself, others or the world. I demand an easy, fair world and pleasant events so that I can adjust and live with calmness."

DISPUTE YOUR IRRATIONAL BELIEF
UNTIL
YOU NO LONGER BELIEVE IT.

HAPPINESS DOESN'T DEPEND UPON
WHO YOU ARE
OR WHAT YOU HAVE;
IT DEPENDS SOLELY UPON WHAT YOU THINK.*

* Dale Carnegie

Many people, including therapists, find *The Serenity Prayer* inspirational for attempting to change bad things and for accepting bad things which cannot be changed.

```
 o                                                    o
             GOD GRANT ME
   SERENITY TO ACCEPT THE THINGS I CANNOT CHANGE,
       COURAGE TO CHANGE THE THINGS I CAN,
                    AND
        WISDOM TO KNOW THE DIFFERENCE.*
 o                                                    o
```

* The Serenity Prayer was probably written by Reinhold Niebuhr. Some credit St. Francis of Assisi with writing it.

```
 o                 Grant me                          o
          serenity (calmness) to accept
    (to tolerate without demanding it must not be) the things
 (my practical problems, adversities, and resistive emotional problems)
               I cannot change,
      courage (determination) to change the things
 (my practical problems, adversities, and emotional problems) I can,
                    and
        wisdom to know the difference.*
 o                                                    o
```

* The Serenity Prayer with Rational Emotive Behavior Therapy interpretation, by Lynn Clark

Therapy is often helpful in accomplishing personal change, in achieving change more quickly, and in determining what can and what cannot be changed. Some emotional problems and disorders are resistive to change.

Advice From Therapists

- *"Accept the world as it is, without demanding how it must be, and awfulizing when it isn't. Strive to accept reality without being passive, condoning, or resigning yourself to disliked parts of your world"* (Dryden & Neeman, p. 52, 1994).

- *"You largely, not completely, create your [self-defeating] disturbances and have the constructive ability to minimize them and actualize yourself. Use that ability"* (Ellis in Weinrach, 1996).

- *"Minimize your demandingness [the three musts] and awfulizing, raise your frustration tolerance, and accept yourself and others as fallible human beings"* (Dryden in Weinrach, 1996).

- *"Be courageous in changing those things that you can change, calmly accept those that you can't, and have the wisdom to know the difference"* (Bernard in Weinrach, 1996).

Chapter 11, More Ways To Help Ourselves, presents suggestions for a person interested in seeking professional help. The chapter also states that medication along with therapy is often beneficial.

With effort from you, SOS will teach you methods to achieve *effective rational beliefs and manage your emotions. You* need to read, study the exercises, practice the various self-help methods, and apply what you have learned to your situation and life. *Maintaining a system of rational beliefs takes continuing attention and effort.*

> YOU ARE RESPONSIBLE
> FOR MANAGING YOUR EMOTIONS

Main Points To Remember:

- Rational beliefs, as opposed to irrational beliefs, are logical, reality-based, useful, helpful for our emotions, based on preferences and wishes, and lack the five hot links.

- Detect, dispute, and uproot your irrational beliefs and self-talk which mainly cause your anxiety, anger, or depression.

- Dispute and debate your irrational belief until you no longer believe it.

- To get in touch with your self-talk and feelings, ask yourself three questions:
  "What am I saying to myself about myself?"
  "What am I saying to myself about others?"
  "What am I saying to myself about this unpleasant situation?"

- Since low frustration tolerance (LFT) is a major cause of emotional disturbance, work on increasing your ability to bear frustration.

- The more you are frustrated, by unfair people and events, the more you need to improve your ability to bear frustration. This is especially true in times of crisis.

- When you're upset, complete the *ABCDE Self-Analysis And Improvement Form* to better understand and manage your emotions.

- Post and learn the Serenity Prayer.

> GRANT ME
> SERENITY TO ACCEPT THE THINGS I CANNOT CHANGE,
> COURAGE TO CHANGE THE THINGS I CAN,
> AND WISDOM TO KNOW THE DIFFERENCE.

Chapter 6

Common Irrational Beliefs And Self-Talk

NURTURING IRRATIONAL BELIEFS

People resist changes to their irrational beliefs. Some people defend, nurture, care for, and feed their irrational beliefs.

Chapter Five, Uprooting Our Irrational Beliefs And Self-Talk, describes how to successfully dispute and uproot irrational beliefs after detecting and identifying them.

In this chapter you'll learn:

- *eleven common irrational beliefs and self-talk statements* to detect and uproot.

• *secondary emotional problems* and how to avoid them, and

• types of *cognitive distortions and thinking errors* which cause emotional problems

Major Musts And Hot Links Underlie Other Irrational Beliefs

Irrational beliefs and self-talk cause us considerable anxiety, anger, and depression. Core irrational beliefs are the *three major musts and shoulds, and the five hot connecting links*.

As you read, recognize that these underlying musts, shoulds, and hot links cause additional irrational beliefs, including the *eleven common irrational beliefs, cognitive distortions*, and *thinking errors*.

Let's briefly review musts, shoulds, and hot links since they are fundamental to our other irrational beliefs and are so basic in causing unhappiness.

Three Major *Musts*: Irrational Self-Talk

1.   *I MUST ...!*

2.   *You (he or she) MUST ...!*

3.   *The world and the conditions under which I live MUST ...!*

Musts, must nots, absolute shoulds, should nots, oughts, and *have to* are all harmful beliefs and self-talk statements when used as absolute demands on oneself, others, the world, and the conditions under which one lives. An easily annoyed physician believed, *"I have to be the best in everything I do."* An exhausted mother believed, *"I've gotta be a perfect mother all the time."*

Five Hot Connecting Links:
Connecting Our Major Musts To Our Emotions

1. **Condemnation & Damnation.***
   Wishing punishment and ruin on yourself or others results in anger directed toward yourself or others. *"You *§æ!±»! louse!"* and *"You SOB!"* are examples.

2. **I-can't-stand-it-itis.**
   I can't stand any discomfort, anxiety, anger, or depression. I can't survive or be happy at all if I have to endure these feelings. I absolutely refuse to accept feeling uncomfortable. This irrational self-talk causes LFT – Low Frustration Tolerance.

3. **Awfulizing.**
   This situation is more than 100% awful; it is HTA - horrible, terrible, awful. *Horribleizing, terribleizing,* and *catastrophizing* are similar to awfulizing.

4. **I'm Worthless.**
   I'm no good at all. Low Self-Acceptance (LSA), low self-esteem, and depression result from this irrational self-talk and thinking. *"I'm a no good RP (rotten person)!"* is an example.

5. **Always & Never.**
   He, she, or the situation will always be this way and will never change.

WHEN YOU ARE UPSET,
LOOK FOR HOT LINKS IN YOUR SELF-TALK

---

* Technical Talk: The five hot connecting links are termed "irrational conclusions" or "derivatives from major musts" in rational emotive behavior therapy (Ellis, 1994).

The five hot links connect "musts" and "shoulds" to our emotions. These irrational beliefs (hot links, musts, shoulds), if not uprooted or managed, will create unhappiness, anxiety, anger, depression, and self-defeating behavior. Use "CIA, IA" to remember the hot links.

CIA, IA – Code For Hot Links

C	Condemnation & Damnation
I	I-can't-stand-it-itis
A	Awfulizing
I	I'm Worthless
A	Always & Never

Eleven Common Irrational Beliefs

Rational emotive behavior therapists (Ellis, 1994; Ellis & Lang, 1994) have identified eleven commonly held irrational beliefs and self-talk statements. By holding on to these irrational beliefs, individuals cause themselves considerable anxiety, anger, depression, and other kinds of emotional distress. These beliefs are responsible for much self-defeating behavior and failure to attain important goals.

Most of the eleven common irrational beliefs (to be described shortly) are caused by the underlying *major musts, absolute shoulds*, and *five hot links*.

People in most all cultures upset themselves in endless ways by demanding that the world be the way they want it to be. Strive for positive change in your life and in the lives of others, but don't unduly disturb yourself by escalating your wishes and preferences into absolute demands coupled with hot links.

```
┌────────────────────────────────────────────┐
│ ○                                        ○   │
│     KNOW HOW TO SOOTHE YOUR EMOTIONS,        │
│         WHEN YOU ARE UPSET.                  │
│ ○                                        ○   │
└────────────────────────────────────────────┘
```

Reflect on the following illogical ideas and then select three or four which come closest to applying to you. At an emotional level, which three or four irrational beliefs are you most tempted to endorse? For additional practice, think about various individuals you know. In which of these irrational beliefs do you think a particular friend, co-worker, or relative might believe?

Make a note of the irrational beliefs which, in part, might apply to you. Work at disputing and uprooting those beliefs causing you to feel anxious, angry, or depressed.

Eleven Irrational Beliefs And Self-Talk Statements

 # 1. It is a dire necessity for me to be loved or approved by almost all others, who are significant to me. And if I am not, as I must be, then it's awful, I-can't-stand-it, I'm worthless.

A young psychology professor once told me, "*It came as real shock to me when I found out that not all of my students liked me.*" Emotionally, he eventually accepted this discovery, after a period of time, and continued being an effective teacher who was liked by most of his students.

Typical Consequences – Low self-acceptance, low self-esteem, anxiety, depression.

Rational Alternative Beliefs – *I prefer to be liked and approved by most people who are significant to me. Knowing that everyone doesn't like or approve of me isn't awful, I-can-stand-it, and I can still feel worthwhile. It isn't reasonable to expect everyone to approve of me. I have little control over how other people think and feel.*

 # 2. I must be thoroughly competent, adequate, and achieving in all important respects, in order to be worthwhile.
I must be 100% competent in all important areas and if I am not as I must be, its awful, I-can't-stand-it, I'm worthless, and I should be condemned.

Typical Consequences – Anxiety, depression, low self-acceptance, low self-esteem, procrastination.
Rational Alternative Beliefs – *I'm an imperfect, fallible person who has both strengths and limitations.* * *I will work toward improving myself. There are things I do well. I can learn from my mistakes and from the hard knocks of life.*

 # 3. The world must be fair. People must act fairly and considerately and if they don't, they are bad, wicked, villainous, or incredibly stupid; they should be severely blamed and punished.
The world and others must be fair. If others are not fair, it's awful, I-can't-stand-it, and they should be condemned & damned; they will always be that way and they will never change unless they acknowledge that they are bad, wicked, or stupid.

Typical Consequences – Anger, rage, seeking of revenge.
Rational Alternative Beliefs – *I'd prefer that others and the world be fair and reasonable, but life often isn't fair. When possible, I will press others to behave fairly.*
Some people believe that they must always act fairly and do the right thing – and then severely blame and condemn themselves for not being perfect. They need to forgive themselves, to regret their behavior, and to work toward doing better in the future. If they are unable to forgive themselves, they may develop considerable guilt and depression.

---

* Interested in obtaining, *"I'm A Fallible Human Being"* T-shirt? Ask for a catalog from Albert Ellis Institute For Rational Emotive Behavior Therapy, 45 East 65th Street, New York, NY 10021. <http://www.rebt.org>

4. <u>The world must be easy</u>. It's awful and terrible when things are not the way I very much want them to be.

Things must be the way I want them to be and if they are not, its awful, I-can't-stand-it, the world should be damned & condemned, I'm worthless, and I'll never be happy.

<u>Typical Consequences</u> - Depression, anxiety, anger.

<u>Rational Alternative Beliefs</u> – *I'd prefer that things go the way that I want them to go. Sometimes things go my way and sometimes they don't. When things don't go my way, it's inconvenient or bad, but not awful. I don't like it, but I can stand it. I can't always control events around me; I can mainly control my beliefs and self-talk about those events, and thereby, control my feelings to a large extent.*

*I can desire, pray, work toward, "Serenity (calmness) to accept (to tolerate without demanding <u>it must not be</u>) the things (my practical problems, adversities, and resistive emotional problems) I cannot change, courage (determination) to change the things (my practical problems, adversities, and emotional problems) I can, and wisdom to know the difference."**

Correct Straight A—B—C Thinking

A ——— Activates ——— B ——— Causes ———> C

A	B	C
Activating Event	Beliefs & Self-Talk	Consequences: Emotional & Behavioral

---

5. There isn't much I can do about my anxiety, anger, depression, or unhappiness, because my feelings are caused by what happens to me.

Believing that other people, events, and situations <u>mainly</u> <u>cause</u> one's feelings is irrational, crooked thinking. This kind of thinking is shown in the next illustration.

---

* The Serenity Prayer with Rational Emotive Behavior Therapy interpretation, by Lynn Clark

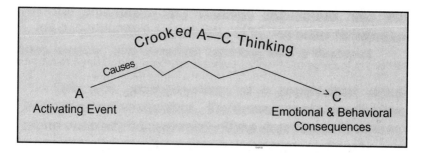

It is often difficult to control one's emotions. However, it's less difficult after SOS shows you specific methods and techniques for doing so.

<u>Typical Consequences</u> – Unhappiness, emotional turmoil, fear, and panic resulting from one's emotions and behavior seemingly being out of control.
<u>Rational Alternative Belief</u> – *What I believe and tell myself about events and situations mainly causes my feelings.*

6. If something is dangerous or dreadful, I should be constantly and excessively upset about it and should dwell on the possibility of its occurring.

One woman frequently stayed alone because her husband had a job requiring travel. She usually didn't "check to see" that her doors were locked at night, saying she was too scared to check. Fear and irrational beliefs prevented her from taking reasonable precautions.

<u>Typical Consequences</u> – Anxiety, fear, worry, difficulty sleeping, mental exhaustion.

A related irrational belief is as follows:
Many situations are dangerous (physically threatening or holding a high likelihood of rejection by others), and I must constantly be alert to avoid dangerous situations.

Rational Alternative Beliefs – Most potentially dangerous situations don't actually occur. I can be cautious and control dangerous events to some extent. I can handle and adjust to the bad things I cannot change.

7. It's easier to avoid and to put off facing life's difficulties and responsibilities than to face them.

It's awful and I-can't-stand the frustration of dealing with situations and hassles that I should not have to deal with. Difficulties and hassles should be condemned and damned.

Typical Consequences – Procrastination and guilt result; small problems turn into large problems; one feels overwhelmed with multiplying difficulties; one's major goals become jeopardized; self-defeating behavior results; often anxiety and depression result. People who believe #7 frequently have low ability to bear frustration.

A related irrational belief is as follows:

I must get really upset or angry before taking action to correct a difficult, unpleasant situation.

I must wait until a difficult situation becomes intolerable or until I get really upset before I do something about that situation. I have to wait until I-can't-stand-it anymore, before I:

- contact a noisy neighbor.
- ask for a change in my job or for a raise.
- tell a friend I don't like the way he or she treated me.
- get my children to improve their behavior in public.
- talk to the teacher about my grade.
- exchange a defective product.

Rational Alternative Beliefs – *Dealing with responsibilities, hassles, and chores is a part of life. Attending to problems in their early stages is inconvenient but hardly awful. I-can-stand dealing with problems as they occur.*

 # 8. I'm quite dependent on others and need someone stronger than myself to rely upon; I cannot run my own life.

I must have someone stronger to depend upon, and if I don't, it's awful, I-can't-stand-it, I'm worthless, and I'll always be miserable. I'm helpless and can't function without considerable help from others.

Typical Consequences – Dependency on others who are not dependable in meeting one's needs; anxiety.

Rational Alternative Beliefs – *I would like for others to guide and support me, but it's more realistic to rely upon myself. I can learn to be more independent.*

 # 9. My past history mainly causes my present feelings and behavior; things from my past which once strongly influenced me will always strongly influence me.

Typical Consequences – The person who maintains this belief may be awash in unpleasant feelings and emotions and give up trying to improve those feelings and emotions.

A related irrational belief is as follows:
When a person is emotionally disturbed, there is almost always a specific cause in the person's past. When that cause is found, understood, and dealt with, the person will no longer be disturbed.

One's past, especially traumatic events and severe childhood stress, is important and can contribute to a person's current disturbance. However, repeatedly re-indoctrinating oneself with irrational beliefs (some of which are conscious, some unconscious, and some from childhood) is what mainly disturbs a person. The person who is upset needs to identify and uproot the irrational beliefs causing the emotional upsetness.

In therapy, an individual holding the irrational belief related to #9 often finds that he does not feel better after discovering the presumed cause of his emotional problems. Rarely is there a single, distant, hidden cause which is responsible for an individual's high level of anxiety, anger, or depression.

The causes of one's problems frequently lie in one's continuing irrational beliefs and self-talk. Therapy can help to detect and dispute these beliefs and lead to improved mood and behavior.

Psychoanalysis and parts of the media and popular culture have fostered the belief that, once an individual has been strongly influenced by a traumatic event (especially an event occurring in childhood), the person will always be strongly influenced. Most, but not all people, recover from traumatic events. Emotional recovery from traumatic events is undoubtedly related to what people believe and tell themselves about the traumatic event.

Long term, continuing trauma in childhood (such as repeated sexual abuse) or a childhood devoid of love and nurturing can have a powerful negative influence on developing children. However, most children from this background do go on to develop normally as adults, although they retain some bad memories. Individuals from a tragic childhood, who believe that people from a tragic childhood usually have emotional problems in adult life, are at increased risk for developing emotional problems.

Rational Alternative Beliefs – *My current feelings and behavior are controlled more by my current beliefs and self-talk than by distant events occurring many years ago. Some parts of my past are unpleasant, but I can learn to live with them; and I have learned from these experiences. I can learn ways to be less upset about unpleasant parts of my past.*

10.I must become very anxious, angry, or depressed over someone else's problems and disturbances, if I care about that person.

Others whom I care about must not be significantly troubled and miserable and if they are, as they absolutely must not be, its awful, I-can't-stand-it, I'm worthless, and it will always be this way. I must not be happy knowing that others are miserable.

<u>Typical Consequences</u> – Anxiety, depression, anger.

One unhappy person asked, *"How can anyone be happy while there is so much tragedy in the world?"* It's true that there is a lot of misery in the world and bad things often happen to good people. It's one of my values to help others and to work toward building a better world. However, a person can become so emotionally upset over the misfortunes and problems of others that he becomes dysfunctional in his own life and ineffective in helping others.

"I love Mother so much ...."

Away at college, Mike was miserable because he loved his mother a great deal and she was deeply depressed.

Mike spent much time thinking of something that would show his mother how much he cared. *"I love mother so much. If I died myself, and left her a letter saying how much I cared for her, then she would know how much I love her! And she would know that I understood what she was going through."*

Mike was continuously re-indoctrinating himself in irrational belief #10. Although he wasn't clearly aware of it, he was also saying to himself, *"Mother must not be depressed and despondent and if she is as she absolutely must not be, its awful, I-can't-stand-it, I'm worthless, and she will always feel miserable."*

After several therapy sessions Mike became aware of how maladaptive his irrational beliefs and thoughts about possibly ending his life were. He started managing his emotions better, and he developed a rational plan for providing his mother with emotional support.

Rational Alternative Beliefs – *I am concerned and saddened when bad things happen to others, and I will work toward helping them, if I'm able. However, the misfortune and unhappiness of others cannot <u>directly</u> cause me to feel extreme anxiety, depression, or unhappiness.*

> WHEN YOU ARE UPSET,
> LOOK FOR THE MUST, LOOK FOR THE SHOULD!

11. There is a right and perfect solution to almost all problems, and it's awful not to find it.

There should be a right and perfect solution, and I must find it. If not, it's awful; I-can't-stand-it; the problem should be damned; and there will never be any solution.

Typical Consequences – Anxiety, anger, and depression; constantly thinking about problems.

Rational Alternative Beliefs – *I don't like problems without perfect solutions, but I can live with them. I can influence, but not entirely control, my world which is complicated and often frustrating.*

> UNFULFILLED PREFERENCES, WISHES, AND DESIRES
> CAN'T MAKE US MISERABLE.
> ABSOLUTE DEMANDS, MUSTS, AND SHOULDS CAN.

Eleven Common Irrational Beliefs
Causing Emotional Distress

#1.   It is a dire necessity for me to be loved or approved by almost all others, who are significant to me.

#2.   I must be thoroughly competent, adequate, and achieving, in all important respects, in order to be worthwhile.

#3.   The world must be fair. People must act fairly and considerately and if they don't, they are bad, wicked, villainous, or incredibly stupid; they should be severely blamed and punished.

#4.   The world must be easy. It's awful and terrible when things are not the way I very much want them to be.

#5.   There isn't much I can do about my anxiety, anger, depression, or unhappiness, because my feelings are caused by what happens to me.

#6.   If something is dangerous or dreadful, I should be constantly and excessively upset about it and should dwell on the possibility of its occurring.

#7.   It's easier to avoid and to put off facing life's difficulties and responsibilities than to face them.

#8.   I'm quite dependent on others and need someone stronger than myself to rely upon; I cannot run my own life.

#9.   My past history mainly causes my present feelings and behavior; things from my past which once strongly influenced me will always strongly influence me.

#10. I must become very anxious, angry, or depressed over someone else's problems and disturbances, if I care about that person.

#11. There is a right and perfect solution to almost all problems, and it's awful not to find it.

Secondary (Additional) Emotional Problems: How To Avoid Creating Them

A secondary emotional problem is further upsetting and disturbing yourself about being upset and disturbed (Ellis, 1994, pp. 253-254; Dryden & Neenan, 1994).

For example, suppose that on Monday morning you are to give a speech or presentation at work or school.* All weekend you obsess, worry, and upset yourself about giving this brief speech. This obsessing, worrying, and upsetting yourself is the primary emotional problem.

You observe your emotional upsetness and on Sunday you tell yourself, *"I must not get so upset about giving a simple speech and since I am so upset, I'm worthless; I should be condemned & damned; I'll always be this way; and I'll never improve in speech making!"* The emotional consequence of this irrational self-talk is depression on Sunday. Sunday depression becomes a secondary (additional) emotional problem.

Sunday depression is a secondary emotional problem because it comes second and follows the primary emotional problem of worrying about giving the speech.

---

* Technical Talk: The *ABC View Of Our Secondary Emotional Problems* is as follows. Anxiety and worry about a scheduled presentation on Monday become an Activating Event. Beliefs & Self-Talk include, *"I must not get so upset about giving a simple presentation, and since I am so upset, I'm worthless; I should be condemned & damned; I'll always be this way; and I'll never improve!"* The Emotional & Behavioral Consequences include Sunday depression and feelings of worthlessness.

Note that major musts and hot links are also active in generating secondary as well as primary emotional problems.

A—B—C View Of Our Secondary Emotional Problems

A — Activates/Triggers —	B — Causes — >	C
Activating Event 2	Beliefs & Self-Talk 2	Emotional & Behavioral Consequences 2
Observing your emotional upsetness.	What you tell yourself about your observed emotional upsetness.	Anxiety or depression about your observed emotional upsetness.

What are other examples of secondary emotional problems? If you are depressed (primary emotional problem) about something, you further depress yourself (secondary emotional problem) about your depression. You might do this by saying to yourself, *"Only a weak and worthless person becomes depressed, and since I am depressed, I am really a weak and worthless nothing ..."*

If you are anxious and fearful (primary emotional problem) about taking a math exam, you further upset yourself by becoming depressed (secondary emotional problem) about your math anxiety.

UPSETTING YOURSELF ABOUT BEING UPSET:
CREATING SECONDARY EMOTIONAL PROBLEMS

"I've gotten very depressed about my phobias. And lately, I've become anxious about my depression."

Be careful what you tell yourself about your unpleasant feelings. Don't create additional emotional problems for yourself.

When you become anxious, angry, or depressed about a situation, be careful that you don't further upset yourself *about* being anxious, angry, or depressed. When upset and distressed about something, listen to what you are telling yourself about that upsetness and distress. A good way to determine if you have a secondary emotional problem is to ask yourself, *"How do I feel about being depressed (or anxious)? What does that say about me, that I often have trouble feeling depressed?"*

Secondary emotional problems are very common. Avoid creating one for yourself! Learn to soothe your emotions rather than creating a second set of negative emotions.

Useful self-talk to combat feeling upset about having emotional problems is, *"I'm not a perfect person. I'm fallible with strengths and weaknesses just like other people. I will try not to further upset myself about my upsetness."*

THE ROAD TO MAJOR FAILURES IN LIFE
IS PAVED WITH
IRRATIONAL SELF-TALK & BELIEFS

TO STRAIGHTEN OUT YOUR EMOTIONS,
FIRST STRAIGHTEN OUT
YOUR BELIEFS AND SELF-TALK

Cognitive Distortions And Thinking Errors*
To Avoid

Cognitive distortions and thinking errors further explain how people needlessly upset themselves. The terms cognitive distortions and thinking errors have the same meaning but many therapists prefer the term "thinking errors" because it sounds less intimidating.

Cognitive refers to thoughts, beliefs, and self-talk. When our thoughts and self-talk statements become distorted and full of errors, we cause ourselves major emotional distress, such as continuing anger and irritableness.

We all make these thinking errors to a greater or lessor extent. But people who habitually make these errors cause themselves considerable misery and anguish.

Let's take a closer look at these automatic thoughts and thinking errors which cause so much emotional distress. *An automatic thought is a rapid, spontaneous mental interpretation of an event or situation with the interpretation leading to an emotional response.* Automatic thoughts are like beliefs and self-talk statements in that they are spontaneous and only partly in our conscious awareness.

Many of our automatic thoughts are irrational. *Irrational automatic thoughts lead to cognitive distortions and thinking errors. These errors are misinterpretations of events and situations and cause irrational emotional responses and exaggerations of emotional responses.*

---

* Technical Talk: *Cognitive distortions and thinking errors* are helpful concepts from Aaron Beck (Beck & Rush, 1995), David Burns (1999), and others. To gain a deeper understanding of cognitive distortions and thinking errors, consider reading a book by David Burns, *Feeling Good: The New Mood Therapy* (1999).

Both cognitive therapy (CT) and rational emotive behavior therapy (REBT) agree that thoughts and self-talk are the primary cause of emotions.

For many people, these cognitive distortions and thinking errors constantly repeat themselves and cause self-defeating behavior and emotional problems. They block our happiness and intensify our anxiety, anger, and depression. These thinking errors limit our ability to understand the feelings of others and to manage relationships.

With effort and study we can learn to be aware of our automatic thoughts. More importantly, we can learn to control them and limit their negative impact on our emotions.

You can attempt to discover if you are making certain thinking errors by studying alone, with the help of a therapist, or with the assistance of a therapy group. If there is no evidence supporting the validity of a particular thought, you need to repeatedly and forcefully attempt to persuade yourself that the thought is false, thus reducing the influence of that thought on your emotion, mood, and behavior.

The following section introduces common types of cognitive distortions and thinking errors (Hales & Hales, 1995). Which of these ten thinking errors might you be making?

Cognitive Distortions And Thinking Errors

1. **All-or-nothing thinking** – You see an event, situation, or person as either black-or-white with no shades of gray. When competing at school or work, if he doesn't come in first, an individual might believe he is a failure.

2. **Overgeneralization** from bad events – You take one bad example or event, generalize from it, and believe that all other similar examples or events will also be bad.

3. **Negative mental filter** filters in only negative examples – Your thinking only accepts the negative examples of something. Consequently, all that you see or remember are the bad examples or experiences.

4.   Disqualifying positive examples – You quickly discount, reject, or minimize positive examples of something. For example, a depressed parent might think that her positive qualities as a parent really aren't important and shouldn't be considered or counted.

5.   Mind reading others' thoughts – We impulsively interpret someone's reaction to us as negative and believe that they don't like us without evidence for this judgment. This is jumping to conclusions.

> **Fortune telling & predicting bad events** –
> We impulsively predict that an event or person will
> disappoint us, and we act accordingly, without
> evidence for this prediction. This is jumping to
> conclusions.

6.   Magnification of negative examples – This is magnifying the importance of a bad event, mistake, or personal characteristic.   A person may have a small, barely noticeable blemish on her face and exaggerate its importance.

> **Minimization of positive examples** – This is
> minimizing the importance of a positive event or
> personal success. A depressed child might earn all
> "B's" in school and then claim any classmate could
> have done it. Or the depressed child's parent might
> say any child could easily get all "B's."

7.   Emotional reasoning overrules logical reasoning– This is reasoning with your feelings alone and without logic or evidence. A person might feel unappreciated and unloved by her family when in fact her family appreciates and loves her.   Other examples of this thinking error include:

> • *"I feel deeply depressed; therefore I must be*
>   *worthless."*
> • *I feel angry at her; therefore that proves she*
>   *is treating me badly."*
> • *"I am afraid of that gerbil; therefore it really is*
>   *dangerous!*

8. Shoulds and musts – You make demands on yourself, others, and the world (or the conditions under which you live) using absolute shoulds, musts, must nots, and oughts. You demand that others and the world give you your way and give you what you want.

9. Negative Labeling of self & others – This is calling yourself or others such names as: "a failure," "a screw-up," "an idiot," "a loser" or "*§æ!±»!" Do evaluate your behavior, but avoid calling yourself and other people names in your silent self-talk. Avoid the hot link of condemnation & damnation.

10. Blaming only one's self or **blaming only others** – This is giving total blame either to yourself or to others for some bad event. Most unpleasant events are caused by a combination of factors.

Cognitive Distortions And Thinking Errors

1. All-or-nothing thinking
2. Overgeneralization from bad events
3. Negative mental filter – filters in only negative examples
4. Disqualifying the positive examples
5. Mind reading others' thoughts **and Fortune telling**
6. Magnification of negative examples **and Minimization** of positive examples
7. Emotional reasoning overrules logical reasoning
8. Shoulds and musts
9. Negative labeling of self & others
10. Blaming only self or **blaming only others**

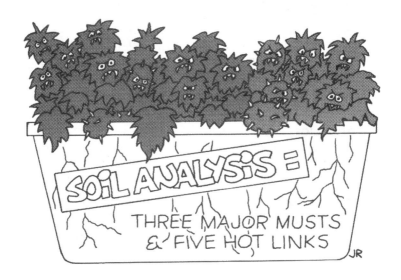

THE THREE MAJOR MUSTS AND FIVE HOT LINKS
PROVIDE FERTILE SOIL FOR:
ELEVEN COMMON IRRATIONAL BELIEFS,
SECONDARY EMOTIONAL PROBLEMS,
COGNITIVE DISTORTIONS, AND THINKING ERRORS.

The Three Major Musts are absolute demands on oneself, others, and the world.

They include: *I MUST ...! You (he or she) MUST ...! The world and the conditions under which I live MUST ...!* Musts also include, must nots, absolute shoulds, should nots, and oughts.

The Five Hot Links (which combine with the Three Major Musts) include: Condemnation & Damnation, I-can't-stand-it-itis, Awfulizing, I'm Worthless, and Always & Never.

When joined together, the Major Musts and Hot Links create 11 Common Irrational Beliefs, Secondary Emotional Problems, Cognitive Distortions, and Thinking Errors. All of these irrational beliefs produce intensified anxiety, anger, depression, shame, excessive guilt, jealousy, and envy.

Main Points To Remember:

• The five hot links (*condemnation & damnation, I-can't-stand-it-itis, awfulizing, I'm worthless,* and *always & never*), when <u>combined</u> <u>with</u> "musts" and "shoulds," can cause continuing emotional distress. Use "CIA, IA" to remember the hot links.

• From the hot links, musts, and shoulds, grow eleven common irrational beliefs.

• Review the eleven common irrational beliefs. Ask yourself, *"Of the eleven irrational beliefs, which three or four are most likely to apply to me, to some extent?"*

• Be careful what you tell yourself <u>about</u> your anxiety, anger, or depression. You could be causing yourself a *secondary (additional) emotional problem.*

• *When you are upset, look for the <u>must</u>, look for the <u>should</u>!*

• *Unfulfilled preferences, wishes, and desires can't make us miserable. Absolute demands, musts, and shoulds can.*

• Cognitive distortions and thinking errors are irrational thoughts which cause emotional distress and maladaptive behavior.

• Test your understanding of Chapters Four, Five, and Six. Turn to Chapter 12 and complete Part Two of the quizzes and exercises.

Part Three

MANAGING ANXIETY, ANGER AND DEPRESSION

Chapter 7

Managing Anxiety

Help! Help!

Some activating events, such as being chased by someone with a weapon, are a concrete and powerful cause of fear!

There's a difference between fear and anxiety. Fear mainly results from a specific, present threat or danger, as shown in the above chase. Anxiety is triggered by future threats to our well-being, threats which are vague and poorly defined.

The primary causes of our anxiety are our beliefs and self-talk.

In this chapter we'll consider:

• the difference between anxiety as a problem and anxiety as a disorder;

• types of anxiety disorders;

• causes of anxiety, such as irrational self-talk and threats of losing something valuable (like our health or an important relationship); and

• ways to prevent and manage anxiety.

We all have difficulties and problems in living. If our practical problems (that is, bad, activating events) and our emotional reactions to these problems become severe enough, we can develop a disorder. The intensity of our reaction determines whether a problem becomes a disorder. *A disorder results when an individual experiences considerable distress or significant impairment in relationships with others or significant impairment as a wage earner, homemaker, or student* (DSM, 2000).*

Webster's dictionary defines *anxiety* as, "a painful or apprehensive uneasiness of mind usually over an impending or anticipated [bad event]....an abnormal and overwhelming sense of apprehension and fear often marked by physiological signs (as sweating, tension, and increased pulse), by doubt concerning the reality and nature of the threat, and by self-doubt about one's capacity to cope with it" (Webster's, 1996).

Anxiety can also be described as, "apprehension, tension, or uneasiness from anticipation of danger, the source of which is largely unknown or unrecognized ....regarded as pathologic when it interferes with effectiveness in living, achievement of desired goals or satisfaction, or reasonable emotional comfort" (Psychiatric Glossary, 1994).* Anxiety can result from the threat of losing something we believe to be essential to our happiness such as an important relationship.

---

* DSM is *The Diagnostic And Statistical Manual Of Mental Disorders, 4th Edition, Text Revision,* 2000 and Psychiatric Glossary is *American Psychiatric Glossary,* 1994 both published by the American Psychiatric Association. Descriptions of anxiety disorders are based on these sources.

Being fallible human beings, we are troubled from time to time with *anxiety problems*. If anxiety becomes severe and causes considerable distress or impairment in our lives, it becomes an *anxiety disorder*.

A LITTLE ANXIETY HELPS TO FOCUS THE MIND, BUT TOO MUCH PARALYZES IT.*

---

*Chinese proverb

Rational emotive behavior therapy (REBT), the basis of SOS, is particularly helpful in treating and preventing anxiety disorders. Antianxiety (anti-anxiety) medication in conjunction with REBT therapy can be particularly useful and is discussed in Chapter 11. However, some types of antianxiety medication can become mildly addictive.

Discuss the need for a medical exam with your physician. Medical conditions alone can contribute to anxiety and anxiety disorder symptoms. Thyroid problems, diabetes, hypoglycemia, some heart conditions, and other physical disorders have symptoms similar to anxiety.

Let's look at different types of anxiety disorders.* As you read, beware of the "psychology student's disease," believing that you might have most of the disorders you are reading about!

Eight Kinds Of Anxiety Disorders

Generalized Anxiety Disorder (GAD) – excessive and unrealistic anxiety, worry, and apprehensiveness experienced in a wide variety of everyday situations and circumstances. Physical symptoms often experienced include restlessness, low energy, difficulty concentrating, irritability, muscle tension, muscle soreness, shortness of

---

* Sources are Wilson, G., Nathan, P., O'Leary, K., & Clark, Lee. (1996) and Neal, F., Davison, G., & Haaga, D. (1996).

breath, heart palpitations, and difficulty sleeping. Frequent areas of worry include family, money, work, and illness.

GAD is one of the most common of the anxiety disorders. Caution is important in everyday living and in meeting the challenges of life. However, significant, continuing anxiety and worry can become a disorder. Causes of GAD include irrational beliefs, irrational self-talk, awfulizing, maintaining a low frustration tolerance, and *what-ifing. What-ifing is asking yourself a lot of "what ifs ..." "What if the car breaks down, what if we arrive late, what if ..."* What-if thinking causes anxiety.

It's a mistake to think that people with an anxiety disorder are "paranoid." They are overly fearful and anxious about dangers inherent in daily living, but they don't believe people are intentionally trying to hurt them or cause them problems. In an effort to reduce painful anxiety, these individuals are at risk for acquiring alcohol and drug problems.

Silent self-talk often includes, "*I must not experience discomfort or danger to my physical or psychological well-being and if I do, it's awful, and I-can't-stand-it.*" Additional irrational beliefs can be: "*Not worrying is foolish and irresponsible; my worrying might ward off danger; by constant worrying, I am bracing myself for future dangers and the discomfort that bad events bring.*"

Two irrational beliefs contributing to GAD and discussed in Chapter Six are the following.

> #6.   **If something is dangerous or dreadful, I should be constantly and excessively upset about it and should dwell on the possibility of its occurring.**

> #4.   **It's awful and terrible when things are not the way I very much want them to be.**

Panic Disorder – sudden, overwhelming anxiety which produces terror and many physical symptoms of intense fear such as rapid heartbeat, dizziness, shortness of breath, numbness, tingling, trembling, hot flashes, chills, and fear of losing self-control, going crazy or dying. The terror often peaks in ten minutes and then subsides.

The individual with a panic disorder usually has no idea what caused his sudden intense fear. On the other hand, a person with cat phobia knows exactly what caused her sudden intense fear, a cat!

For many people, the cause of panic disorder is an overly serious or catastrophic interpretation of their body sensations. For example, a person might notice subtle sensations or changes in his body such as heart rate changes or mild shortness of breath (A, an activating event) and then tell himself that something dangerous may be occurring (B, irrational belief and self-talk). The irrational self-talk (B) causes fear and panic (C, consequences, both emotional and behavioral).

"This may be the end!"

Ashley noted that her heart skipped a couple of beats (activating event) and then said to herself, *"Oh, a heart attack! This may be the end, and it's awful* (silent self-talk)." The emotional and behavioral consequence of that irrational self-talk was terror which then caused her heart to race. Realizing that her heart had skipped beats and was now racing, she said to herself, *"Something is terribly wrong!"* This cycle of terror peaked in about 10 to 15 minutes and left Ashley trembling, weak, exhausted, and wondering when the next attack would strike. Ashley unintentionally caused her panic attacks and was unaware that her self-talk was bringing them on.

Since beliefs and self-talk primarily cause your emotions, it's important to listen closely to what you are telling yourself.

Avoid accidentally hyperventilating when you become fearful or anxious, because this can precipitate or intensify panic attacks. Hyperventilation, breathing too rapidly for a couple of minutes, disturbs the balance of oxygen to carbon dioxide in your body. Hyperventilating will definitely cause intense tingling, dizziness, light-headedness, and most other physical symptoms of an anxiety attack, even in individuals who are not particularly anxious.

Agoraphobia (a'•gor'•a•pho'bia) – intense "anxiety about being in places or situations in which escape might be difficult or embarrassing or in which help may not be available" (Psychiatric Glossary, 1994). Common situations may include being away from home, being in a crowd, sitting in a movie theater, standing in line, traveling in a car, entering tunnels, and crossing bridges.

Individuals with agoraphobia frequently have panic disorder as well. They often fear they may have a panic attack in situations where they might be embarrassed by the attack, or where help might not be available.

Social Phobia (also called Social Anxiety Disorder) – marked and persistent fear and avoidance of social situations in which one might be closely observed by others and thus be rejected, humiliated, or embarrassed. The person does not fear being hurt physically, just being rejected, laughed at, or negatively evaluated by others. Common situations include fear of social events; speaking or eating in public; conversing with members of the opposite sex; and using public rest rooms. Intense physical symptoms of anxiety (sweating, trembling) are often present.

A fundamental behavior is avoidance of social situations. As a result of emotional distress and avoidance behavior, the individual is somewhat impaired in his education or job. Feelings of low self-esteem and low self-acceptance (LSA) contribute to social anxiety disorder. Review the section on low self-acceptance in Chapter Nine.

Irrational beliefs and self-talk can be, "*I must be positively evaluated and accepted by others, and if I am not accepted, as I absolutely must be, it would be awful and I couldn't stand it. Then I would be worthless and never find any happiness at all!*" Additional irrational beliefs can be: "*I must not experience discomfort around others. I must perform well and be positively evaluated by others. If I don't perform well, as I absolutely must do, I'm worthless.*"

Two irrational beliefs contributing to social phobia and discussed in Chapter Six are the following.

#2.   I must be thoroughly competent, adequate, and achieving in order to be worthwhile.

#1.   It is a dire necessity for me to be loved or approved by almost all others who are significant to me.

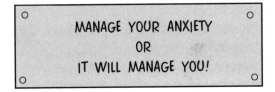

MANAGE YOUR ANXIETY
OR
IT WILL MANAGE YOU!

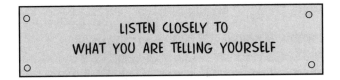

LISTEN CLOSELY TO
WHAT YOU ARE TELLING YOURSELF

To learn more about how our beliefs and self-talk create anxiety and 15 methods to control those beliefs, read *How to control your anxiety before it controls you* by Albert Ellis (1998).

Learning To Manage Anxiety With ABC's

A Activating Event

"I think I'll ask her to go out for a date. I've been thinking about it for two weeks."

Causes

B Beliefs & Self-Talk

"Oh, she might turn me down! If she turns me down, it would be awful, I'd be worthless, and I-couldn't-stand-it!"

C Consequences:
Emotional & Behavioral Consequences

"I can't even think about being turned down. I-can't-stand the discomfort and tension of asking her to go out! I'll wait until next week to ask."

D Dispute

"I'm making myself anxious. If I get turned down, it won't be awful, I-can-stand-it, and I'll work on not feeling worthless. I'm going to ask her to go out."

Specific Phobia – marked and persistent fear that is excessive or unreasonable and triggered by specific objects or situations such as heights, flying, small animals, insects, elevators, seeing blood, or getting an injection. The person experiences marked distress or completely disrupts her life in order to avoid the feared object or situation.

Her self-talk includes, "*I absolutely must not be hurt and if I were, it would be awful and I couldn't stand it! I must not come near fearsome things. I must not experience discomfort around things I am afraid of, and if I do, it would be awful to feel this discomfort and fear!*"

Flying Insect Wrecks Beetle!

Craig, a psychologist, was frightened of flying insects. Once while Craig was driving home from work in his Volkswagen Beetle, an insect flew into his car. He experienced sufficient fear that he lost control of his Beetle and ran off the highway!

Obsessive-Compulsive Disorder (OCD) – frequent, recurrent *obsessions or compulsions* which are severe and time-consuming or cause marked distress or impairment. *Obsessions* are unwelcome recurring thoughts, impulses, or mental images that cause distress. Examples of obsessions would include persistently wondering if a door is locked and thoughts of being contaminated with germs by shaking hands with others.

Compulsions are unwelcome, repetitive actions and behaviors such as frequent hand washing, placing objects in a precise order, frequently checking to see if a door is locked, and repeatedly cleaning the same room. The individual recognizes that the obsessions or compulsions are excessive and unreasonable but, nevertheless, can't control them.

"I Might Contaminate You"

Sally had obsessions about getting germs on her hands and accidentally transferring these germs to others by shaking hands or touching objects, such as a door knob or the arm rest of a chair, that others would later touch. She always felt compelled to wash her hands after touching her shoes. After making purchases she often returned to the store to again tell the surprised clerk, *"Thank you, or if I didn't tell you thank you, then thank you."* for helping with the purchase. Although Sally knew that her obsessions and compulsions were unreasonable, she had much difficulty controlling them.

After six months of cognitive behavior therapy and medication, she regained considerable control over her thoughts and behaviors.

Hypochondriasis (hy•po•chon'•dri•a•sis) – continual worry, anxiety, and unwarranted fear of having a serious disease despite medical reassurance to the contrary. Repeated physical exams, diagnostic tests, and reassurance from a physician do not reduce the individual's worry or convince him that he does not have a threatening illness such as heart disease or cancer.

This persistent worry causes significant emotional distress or impairment in social, family, or vocational functioning. Instead of worrying about family, job, finances, or relationship problems like many people do, the person with hypochondriasis mostly just worries about possible dangers to his body. Physicians report that about 4% to 9% of their patients have hypochondriasis (DSM-IV, 1994).

An irrational belief contributing to hypochondriasis is the following.

#6.   **If something is dangerous or dreadful, I should be constantly and excessively upset about it and should dwell on the possibility of its occurring.**

Adjustment Disorder With Anxiety – following a *severely stressful event or situation* (a bad activating event), the individual develops marked anxiety (extreme nervousness, worry, or jitteriness) and becomes impaired in relationships with others or impaired as a worker, student, or homemaker.

Examples of stressful events include marital conflict, divorce, being fired from a job, failing in school, or losing one's farm or business. Some unfortunate people may experience a couple of these events in the same short period of time. Individuals who normally are untroubled by anxiety can develop *adjustment disorder with anxiety* if they experience very bad events. As one might guess, this disorder is common

ACTIVATING EVENTS PILE UP

"Let's see, ...you lost your job, ...your mother-in-law has come to live with you, ...your car got wrecked, ...and the burglars got most of your furniture! ...I believe your diagnosis is...Adjustment Disorder With Anxiety."

Multiple stressful events can accumulate and strongly contribute to anxiety. However, rational beliefs and self-talk can help us to adjust emotionally and to partially control those bad events.

Rates Of Anxiety Disorders In Adults

Anxiety Disorder	Rates In General Population
Generalized Anxiety Disorder	4% to 7% of Population*
Panic Disorder	2% to 4% of Population*
A•gor•a•pho•bia	2% to 5% of Population**
Social Phobia	11% to 16% of Population*
Specific Phobia	7% to 16% of Population*
Obsessive-Compulsive Disorder (OCD)	2% to 3% of Population**
Hy•po•chon•dri•a•sis	4% to 9% of Medical Patients
Adjustment Disorder With Anxiety	Rates are not known

* Rates of a disorder in the general population over one's lifetime.   **The rates listed for these two disorders are rates in the population at any given time. Unfortunately, an individual can have two disorders at the same time.

Self-Help For
Anxiety Problems And Disorders

When you are feeling worried, tense, or anxious, do the following to interrupt and manage your anxiety and its physical and psychological symptoms.   Chapter Four describes many of these methods and techniques.

- **Acknowledge that beliefs and self-talk mainly cause your emotions** rather than actual events or practical problems (that is, activating events).

- **Deal first with the emotional problem** (your upsetness and anxiety) before attempting to deal with the practical problem or difficult acting-person (the activating event).

- **Replace unhealthy emotions with healthy ones**. Replace fear with concern.

---

* Sources are Wilson, G., Nathan, P., O'Leary, K., & Clark, Lee. (1996) and Neal, F., Davison, G., & Haaga, D. (1996).

• Replace the three major musts and absolute shoulds with preferences and wishes.

• Drop any of the five hot links (condemnation & damnation, I-can't-stand-it-itis, awfulizing, I'm worthless, always & never) that you are using.

• Use emotionally cool language when talking with yourself.

• Use coping self-talk statements such as, *"I don't like it, that's ok, I can stand it anyway."*

• Use distraction, diversion, and entertainment by temporarily becoming involved in some pleasurable activity.

• Practice deep breathing and progressive muscle relaxation when upset. Be sure that you don't accidentally hyperventilate as this will produce or intensify anxiety symptoms.

• Consider having a physical examination, completing a trial period on antianxiety medication, and meeting with a therapist.

To actually get better and to reduce your anxiety over the long term, do the following:

• Use the Anxiety And ABC View Of Our Emotions for understanding and improving your emotions.

• Complete the Anxiety And ABCDE Self-Analysis And Improvement Form.

• Keep a Daily Mood Record to better understand your emotions. Feelings of depression or anger often accompany feelings of anxiety.

• **Detect and identify your irrational beliefs and self-talk** which are mainly responsible for your anxiety.

• **Dispute and talk back to your irrational beliefs and self-talk causing anxiety.** Deepen your conviction as to the destructiveness of your old irrational beliefs and self-talk.

Anxiety And ABC View Of Our Emotions

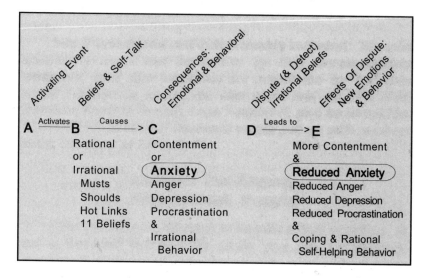

When looking for irrational beliefs which may be causing your anxiety, look over the 11 irrational beliefs in Chapter Six. Especially consider Irrational Belief #6: *If something is dangerous or dreadful, I should be constantly and excessively upset about it and should dwell on the possibility of its occurring.*

Work to overcome both practical problems and emotional problems. However, don't condemn yourself for experiencing continuing painful anxiety or an anxiety disorder. Saying "*I must not have an emotional problem, and if I do I can't-stand-it, I'm worthless and should be damned*" will only intensify your upsetness. This irrational belief and self-talk can cause secondary emotional problems as described in Chapter Six.

Review the *Serenity Prayer* in Chapter Five.

Identify and dispute those self-defeating beliefs and self-talk statements which are mainly responsible for causing your anxiety. The *Anxiety And ABCDE Self-Analysis And Improvement Form* will be helpful for doing this.

Daily Mood Record: Record Of Anxiety, Anger, And Depression				
On a scale from 1 to 10 write in a number corresponding to your estimated average mood for the day. Mild is 1 to 3, moderate is 4 to 5, high is 6 to 8, and severe is 9 to 10.				
Date/ Time	Anxiety	Anger	Depres- sion	Notes

The following directions describe how to keep a Daily Mood Record.

First, decide which of the basic emotions you are going to log. Pay close attention to those emotions. Record your approximate average mood for the emotions you have decided to track. Do this each day. Enter any notes on the record that might help you to better understand your emotions.

Anxiety And ABCDE
Self-Analysis And Improvement Form

                                                        Date:

A <u>Activating</u> <u>Event</u> (Unpleasant event or situation; can be anticipated events):

B <u>Beliefs</u> **And Self-Talk Statements** (Your irrational beliefs and self-talk statements; especially your musts, absolute shoulds, and five hot links):

C <u>Consequences:</u> **Emotional & Behavioral** (Your unpleasant emotion and maladaptive behavior):
Emotions:

Behavior (or contemplated behavior):

D <u>Dispute</u> <u>And</u> <u>Debate</u> (Dispute your irrational beliefs and self-talk; especially your musts, absolute shoulds, and five hot links):

E <u>Effects</u> (Effects Of Dispute: New emotions and behaviors):

Copy this form. Complete the steps in the order of A, C, B, D, and E. When feeling tense and anxious, follow the self-help methods in Chapters 4 and 5.
    As you complete B, look for your musts, absolute shoulds, hot links, and the 11 irrational beliefs described in Chapter Six.

Main Points To Remember:

- *A little anxiety helps to focus the mind, but too much paralyzes it.*

- Anxiety can become more than a problem; it can become a disorder.

- A disorder results when an individual experiences considerable distress, or significant impairment in relationships with others, or significant impairment as a wage earner, homemaker, or student.

- *Manage your anxiety, or it will manage you!*

- When feeling anxious and tense, complete the *Anxiety And ABCDE Self-Analysis And Improvement Form* to better understand and manage your anxiety.

- Use a number of additional SOS self-help methods to deal with your anxiety.

```
 o                                              o
        YOU ARE RESPONSIBLE
      FOR MANAGING YOUR ANXIETY
 o                                              o
```

Chapter 8

Managing Anger

Aristotle, an ancient Greek philosopher who lived 2300 years ago (384-322 B.C.), observed how difficult it is to manage anger.

In this chapter we'll consider: anger as both a problem and a disorder, myths and reality of anger, primary causes of anger, three targets of anger, and methods to get yourself "unangry."

Anger: A Problem And A Disorder

Anger is "*a strong feeling of displeasure and antagonism....synonyms....ire, rage, fury, indignation, wrath mean an intense emotional state induced by displeasure. Anger, the most general term, names the reaction but in itself conveys nothing about the intensity or justification...of the emotional state*" (Webster, 1996).

163

We all are confronted with unpleasant situations and faced with annoying or difficult people. If our angry reaction to situations and people becomes severe enough, we can develop a disorder. *A disorder results when an individual experiences considerable emotional distress or significant impairment in relationships with others or significant impairment as a wage earner, homemaker, or student* (DSM, 2000).* Easily angered individuals typically experience considerable distress or have significant impairment in their social relationships or as a wage earner, homemaker, or student.

In my opinion, feelings of anger usually cause more personal distress than either anxiety or depression. High levels of anger usually lead to limited problem solving ability, impulsive decisions, and foolish actions. It makes us less perceptive of the feelings and thoughts of others. People with an anger problem or disorder, however, are usually reluctant to seek help or to admit that they have a problem.

When we become angry it's important to ask ourselves, "Is the source of my anger within me or in the other person (or the situation)?"

Anger largely results from our irrational beliefs, expectations, and self-talk. Other people can trigger our anger only by activating or stimulating our irrational beliefs. Reduce your anger by uprooting your irrational beliefs and self-talk. *You can't control your anger as long as you believe others cause it. Take responsibility for both creating and reducing your own anger.*

An easily angered person doesn't see the cause of anger as within himself; he attributes his anger to the behavior of others. Matt, having lit his cigarette a couple of minutes earlier, suddenly smashed his fist on the kitchen table. After cooling off, he explained that his wife hadn't noticed the long ash accumulating on his cigarette and had

---

* DSM is *The Diagnostic And Statistical Manual Of Mental Disorders, 4th Edition, Text Revision,* 2000 published by the American Psychiatric Association.
    It does not yet list or describe types of anger disorders as it does for anxiety disorders and depressive disorders.

failed to get him an ashtray! He didn't see himself as having an anger problem. He saw his wife as the problem because she failed to anticipate his need for an ashtray. Matt's irrational beliefs include, *"She must show me she cares by noticing when I need something. If she doesn't, as she should, it's awful and I-can't-stand-it; and why did I get married?"* Easily angered people frequently damage their love relationships.

Individuals with continuing, *strong anxiety or depression* usually admit to themselves that they have an emotional problem or disorder. However, people with continuing, *strong anger* rarely admit that they have an emotional problem. They feel that the problem is solely the external event, situation, or person which triggered their anger. People who believe they have no control over their anger don't.

Anger and other emotional responses are determined primarily by what we believe and tell ourselves about bad events. However, how could someone *not* be lastingly angered and affected by a very bad event such as the murder of a loved one? Let's consider the emotional reactions of family members affected by such a wrongful, tragic event.

"The killer should be found and punished!"

Carla's body was found in the desert long after being murdered by an unknown assailant. Her parents, after grieving for some months, sadly accepted their tragedy without demanding *it must not be.* They began putting their lives back together.

Carla's brother, Mike, however, never accepted her death and endlessly repeated to himself and to others that *"the killer must be found and punished."* He was consumed with anger and obsessed with her unjust death. Mike's friends began avoiding him, and he received poor evaluations at work. He responded by becoming more angry and depressed.

Mike and his parents reacted differently to their tragedy. What they told themselves about her death determined if they accepted the tragedy as painful reality and became saddened, or if they refused to accept it and became consumed with depression and rage.

Mike constantly repeated to himself, *"She shouldn't have been killed. The killer should be found and punished, and if the killer isn't found, it's awful and I-can't-stand-it."* Mike's life was consumed with depression and rage. Of the 11 irrational beliefs, the ones most likely causing his misery are the following. The ones placed first seem to have influenced Mike the most.

#9.   **My past history mainly causes my present feelings and behavior; things from my past which once strongly influenced me will always strongly influence me.**

#5.   **There isn't much I can do about my anxiety, anger, depression, or unhappiness because my feelings are caused by what happens to me.**

#3.   **The world must be fair. People must act fairly and considerately and if they don't, they are bad, wicked, villainous, or incredibly stupid; they should be severely blamed and punished.**

#4.   **It's awful and terrible when things are not the way I very much want them to be.** (The remaining *eleven irrational beliefs* are described in Chapter Six.)

Mike prevented the healing power of *the passage of time* by refusing to accept his sister's death. He constantly reindoctrinated himself with, *"She shouldn't have been killed. ...it's awful and I-can't-stand-it."* Work to change what you can. Ask for serenity to accept what you cannot change.

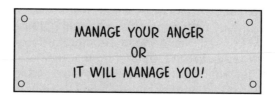

MANAGE YOUR ANGER
OR
IT WILL MANAGE YOU!

Learning To Manage Anger With ABC's

A Activating Event

"And don't call again!"

B Beliefs & Self-Talk

"Why do people do things like that? There should be a law against it. That was very upsetting! That call should have never happened and since it did, it's just awful! I-can't-stand-it"

Causes

C Consequences:
Emotional & Behavioral Consequences

"I am mad as §æ!±»! I hate these <u>telephone solicitation</u> calls. They're as terrible as junk mail and junk faxes! Those §æ!±»! people think I'm a fool and want to waste my time!"

D Dispute

"There I go again, upsetting myself. It's hard to remember, 'It's not the situation that upsets me but it's what I tell myself about it.' That call was inconvenient, but hardly awful. And I need to watch my blood pressure."

Anger: Its Myths And Reality

Several myths perpetuate and reinforce our irrational beliefs about anger and how to manage it (Borcherdt, 1989). Let's look at these myths and the reality.

Myth #1. *"Anger is caused by an event, a situation, or someone else's behavior, all situations outside yourself. People don't have control over their anger; anger is what happens to you."*

Reality. We are responsible for our own anger, both its cause and how it's managed. If we believe we are not responsible for our anger, we will manage it poorly and it will manage us.

The *ABC View Of Our Anger* shows that unpleasant events (and people) only *trigger* our irrational beliefs, and that our beliefs and self-talk actually cause our angry feelings and behavior.*

ABC View Of Our Anger

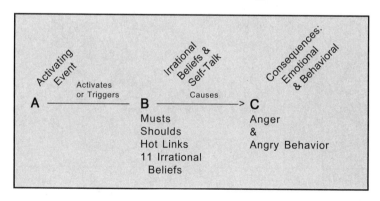

---

* An interesting audiotape, *What Do I Do With My Anger: Hold It In Or Let It Out?* by Raymond DiGiuseppe (1989), is available from Albert Ellis Institute For Rational Emotive Behavior Therapy. <http://www.rebt.org>

Myth #2. *"It's healthy to express your anger. I feel better after I express my anger."*

Reality. Whether we feel angry and express it or feel angry and do not express it, can cause major health problems. Among these are heart disease, high blood pressure (leading to strokes), gastrointestinal symptoms, suppression of our immune system, and other health problems.

Sometimes there is an immediate and pleasant, but brief, release of tension following a strong expression of anger. Anger provides us with a temporary feeling of strength, power, and control and covers up our feelings of hurt, rejection, helplessness, or inadequacy. We feel that we are handling a practical problem (for example, getting a person who is behaving wrongfully to improver her behavior) when we express our anger. An easily angered person who is obsessed with anger is also obsessed with misery.

Myth #3. *"My only two choices regarding my anger are to express it or to hold it in."*

Reality. Actually, there is another choice. Lower, reduce, or turn your anger down instead of expressing it *or* holding it in. Practice turning down your anger by modifying your beliefs and self-talk.

Expressing anger is not getting rid of it. Expressing anger is practicing anger. Practicing anger makes you more likely to express anger when frustrated in the future.

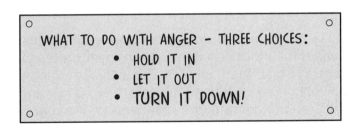

WHAT TO DO WITH ANGER – THREE CHOICES:
- HOLD IT IN
- LET IT OUT
- TURN IT DOWN!

Myth #4. *"Expressing anger gets the attention of others, it gets you what you want, others are less likely to take advantage of you. People need to be confronted about the wrongfulness of their behavior and perhaps be taught a lesson as well."*

Reality. Strongly expressing anger or threatening to express anger often does get you what you want, but usually only in the short run.

In the long run, the strong expression of anger hurts our relationships and invites the recipient of our anger to hold a grudge or retaliate. Eruptions of anger generate resentfulness, bitterness, and distance in relationships. Anger begets anger.

If you are in a position of power over another person and express a lot of anger, you are unlikely to see that person return anger. However, people in a subordinate position often retaliate against anger attacks and do so in hidden ways, sometimes by undermining important goals.

DON'T GET ANGRY, GET ASSERTIVE.

Replace anger with assertiveness and annoyance. Assert and state your feelings or rights without displaying a lot of anger and intense emotion. Be assertive instead of being angry.

Get angry and stupid or get annoyed and insightful. You will think more clearly when annoyed (a less intense emotional state than anger) and solve problems more effectively. The observation, *"People who get angry, get stupid,"* is an accurate one. Manage your anger or it will manage you.

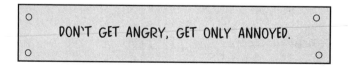

DON'T GET ANGRY, GET ONLY ANNOYED.

ANGER – *HOLD IT IN, OR LET IT OUT?*

"What do I do with my anger, put the lid on it, or let it boil over?" Answer – *"Turn the heat down!"*

You control the intensity of your anger by what you believe and tell yourself about an upsetting or disappointing event or the behavior of another person. Your self-talk and beliefs control your anger like a knob regulates temperature.

Also, as you would temporarily remove a boiling pot from a stove, remove yourself from an especially upsetting situation about to trigger your anger.

Parents often get frustrated with their children. Unfortunately, many parents attempt to manage their children using forms of anger. Parents yell, threaten to lose emotional control, use physical punishment, threaten to severely punish, and use a lot of sarcasm – all ineffective methods for managing children. Children closely observe and imitate the behavior of their parents. If your daughter has observed a lot of anger in you, she is more likely to yell, get emotionally upset, threaten, be sarcastic, and attempt to manage you or others physically.*

Two common sources of our anger are low frustration tolerance and threats to our self-worth. Let's first consider LFT.

Low Frustration Tolerance (LFT): A Prime Source Of Anger

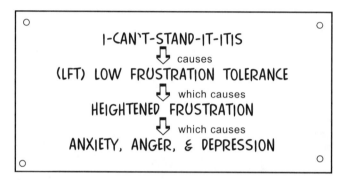

Low frustration tolerance, discussed in Chapter Five and in other sections of SOS, causes many individuals to become angry. Believing that you absolutely must get what you want and if you don't, it's awful and you can't-stand-it causes impatience, low frustration tolerance, heightened frustration, and anger. Replace believing a situation is awful or horrible with believing it's inconvenient or a hassle. When talking with yourself about frustrating situations, use those *cool self-talk words*, "hassle" and "inconvenient."

Common situations triggering LFT include: dealing with uncooperative people, having difficulty with your computer, waiting in a slow line at the checkout counter, sitting in traffic jams, having someone pull out in front of you in traffic, or locking yourself out of the car.

---

* *SOS Help For Parents*, a book for parents of children between the ages of two and twelve, is by Lynn Clark and published by SOS Programs & Parents Press. *SOS Help For Parents* emphasizes the importance of parents consciously being good role models for their children. The book is especially helpful for managing behavior of the strong-willed child. See the end pages of this book and <http://www.sosprograms.com>

Threats To Self-Worth:
A Prime Source Of Anger

Individuals often respond with anger when they perceive that others are attempting to lower their self-worth, self-acceptance, or self-esteem, (Dryden, 1990). The extent of their anger is usually proportional to the extent to which they doubt their own self-worth.

Situations threatening one's self-esteem include: failing to get recognition at school, getting criticism from co-workers or supervisors, and receiving negative comments about one's appearance, possessions, behavior, or ideas.

Work on accepting yourself, and recognize that your rising anger may be due to your feelings of self-worth being threatened. Strive to believe, *"My basic feelings of self-acceptance and self-worth are largely independent of the remarks and thoughts of others."*

Anger can be directed at any of three targets: self, others, and the world (Dryden, 1990). The world includes *the circumstances under which I live*. Let's first look at anger directed toward others.

Three Targets Of Our Anger: Self,
Others, And The World

Anger at others: Anger results from believing, *"You (he or she) MUST and if you don't, then I-can't-stand-it and you should be damned."* Anger is often caused by our perceptions of wrongdoings by others and by believing that they *must not* behave wrongly. Seeing others as frustrating us or threatening our self-esteem are common triggers for our anger.

The people with whom we are most likely to get angry are family members, friends, individuals with whom we are romantically involved, co-workers, supervisors, teachers, and others close to us.

Avoid displacing your anger onto a blameless person. *Displaced anger is feeling angry at a particular person or situation while releasing your anger at another innocent party.* An example would be the man who is criticized by his boss, shouts at his wife, who scolds her child, who mistreats the family dog!

People are fallible human beings, and they usually behave the way they choose, not the way we choose for them to behave. People are able to behave wrongly or against our interests, and we generally have little power to influence their behavior. There are few laws which require people to behave a certain way, and these laws are rarely enforced.

Anger at the world and the conditions under which I live: Beliefs causing anger include, *"The world must be fair and easy and if it isn't, it's awful, I-can't-stand-it, and the world should be condemned and damned."*

You hear people saying, *"Getting a flat tire ruined my day,"* or *"My computer wouldn't run, and I-couldn't-stand-it."* When you feel miserable and angry because you are *demanding* that the world give you what you want, consider substituting preferences and wishes for your demands.

When you express a lot of anger at the world, an unintended target of your anger is normally yourself. One man painfully discovered this. Angry at his potbellied stove, he aimed his pistol and fired directly into the open stove. The slug ricocheted and hit him in the stomach. It's common for unbridled anger or anger directed at others or the world to ricochet or backfire. Anger is self-destructive and often "what we send around, comes around" and back to us.

Intense feelings of frustration and anger weaken our patience. We need patience to understand and solve complex problems, such as relationship problems. Strive to adapt and succeed in a fallible world, and avoid upsetting yourself and whining about its faults, errors, and unfairness.

ANGRY AT THE WORLD:
DEMANDING THAT THE WORLD BE FAIR AND EASY

Anger can result from demandingness – demanding that the world be fair and easy and when it isn't, condemning and damning it. Strive for improvements in your life, but avoid <u>demanding</u> that your wishes always be met.

For increased contentment and decreased anger, change your demands for getting what you want into preferences and wishes.

Anger at self: People often place demands on themselves; and when they fail to meet those demands, they condemn and damn themselves. Emily, a college sophomore, felt that she *absolutely must* get an "A" on her history exam. When she missed an "A" by two points, "as she *must not have done*," she turned her anger on herself and consequently felt miserable. Others get angry at themselves for having job status or income below the level they feel they *must have*.

YOU CAN'T CONTROL YOUR ANGER
AS LONG AS YOU BELIEVE OTHERS CAUSE IT.

We can get angry at ourselves when we violate our own rules and standards for conduct and demand that we must not have done so. Guilt results from breaking our moral code and condemning ourselves for doing so. Don't let anger toward yourself and feelings of guilt turn into depression. Instead of becoming angry and depressed, forgive yourself and resolve to try harder in the future.

Replace anger with acceptance of yourself and others as fallible human beings. Acceptance is "the unqualified and nonjudgmental attitude to self and others, as well as an acknowledgment that what exists is bound to exist given the conditions that are present at the moment (Dryden & Neenan, 1994)." Strive for improvements, but accept yourself, others, and the world as fallible.

To live effectively and successfully, make a conscious effort to manage your anger. When attempting to manage your anger, it helps to believe *the world is fallible, others are fallible, and I'm fallible*.

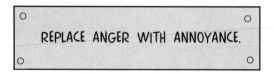

REPLACE ANGER WITH ANNOYANCE.

Triggers For Anger

SELF-WORTH ANGER

"I used to believe that others <u>must</u> <u>never</u> put me down and if they did, <u>I</u> <u>felt</u> <u>worthless</u> and <u>I-couldn't-stand-it</u>. Believing that got me into a lot of fights! I'm working on accepting myself and ignoring what others say or think."

FRUSTRATION AND ANGER

"I regret that I used to physically abuse my wife when I felt frustrated or felt that <u>I</u> <u>must</u> <u>control</u> her. In therapy, I learned to control my anger by accepting that I alone am responsible for my anger and not her."

VALUING TOUGHNESS

"I kinda like getting angry, fighting, and being the toughest girl in school. I have 'reputation' and 'respect.' But I'm afraid I don't have many friends."

Anger is often triggered by our low frustration tolerance or by threats to our self-worth (self-esteem). Our beliefs and self-talk cause our anger rather than what others do or say.

Change your <u>demand</u> that others <u>must</u> do what you want, to a <u>preference</u> or <u>wish</u> that they do what you want. Use these self-talk words with yourself, <u>"wish"</u> and <u>"preference."</u> Your anger will become annoyance, a healthier emotion and easier to manage.

Some people with an anger problem place a positive value on toughness and aggression. As adults, they are at high risk for emotional maladjustment.

NURTURING ANGER

*"I don't think these wounds are ever going to heal...
I keep picking at them and they just don't get any
better ... I kind of like picking at this bottom one."*

People often nourish their anger by repeatedly
reindoctrinating themselves with irrational beliefs
and self-talk and dwelling on the wrongdoings of
others.

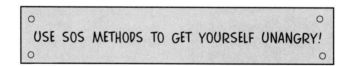

USE SOS METHODS TO GET YOURSELF UNANGRY!

Which person do you think will achieve greater
success in reaching reach his goals in life, Person A or
Person B? Which person would be more likely to experience
continuing conflict with an employer, spouse, or children?

Person A: *"Every day that passes, causes me to
put one more *§æ!±»! on my list of people to get
even with!"*

Person B: *"I am going to learn how to stop
upsetting my self so much by the *§æ!±»! people
I encounter!"*

ANGER – USED AS AN INSTRUMENT
TO GET WHAT YOU WANT

"Get me a Coke! Get me a Coke NOW!"
(from The SOS Video)

Instrumental anger is the anger a person uses as an instrument or lever, to pressure others to give him what he wants. Unfortunately, some parents give in and accidentally reward their child for using anger and emotional upsetness as an instrument for controlling the family and others.

For example, only when Michael expresses increasing anger does mother give in and give him both ice cream and a Coke. Earlier, she had told him *"no dessert"* because he didn't eat his supper.

What is Michael believing and telling himself that causes him to behave aggressively? At a low level of self-awareness, Michael is saying to himself, *"Mother must give me that Coke and if she doesn't, it's awful and I-can't-stand-it! I must have that Coke! I'm going to get real upset, and then she'll give in!"*

Michael has accidentally learned to use emotional upsetness and anger to get what he wants. If this way of thinking and acting becomes a habit, he will be at high risk for experiencing emotional and behavioral problems as an adolescent and adult.

To see a brief video clip of this example (in either English or Spanish) along with solutions parents can implement, go to "Rewarding Bad Behavior" at <www.sosprograms.com>

How To Get Yourself "Unangry"

When feeling angry, examine your self-talk causing your anger. Interrupt and manage your feelings of anger with the following aids, techniques, and ideas.*

- **Acknowledge that your beliefs and self-talk mainly cause your anger** rather than actual events, the wrongdoings of others, frustrating events, or other practical problems (that is, activating events). We are responsible for our own anger.

- **Deal first with your emotional problem** (your upsetness and anger) before attempting to deal with your practical problem (the activating event or person who seems to be angering you).

- **List in two columns the advantages and disadvantages of giving up your anger toward a particular person,** (Burns, 1999).

- **Replace anger and rage** (unhealthy emotions) **with annoyance or mild irritation** (healthier emotions). Replace feeling angry and severely frustrated by an individual with feeling inconvenienced by that individual.

- **Replace anger with assertiveness.** Assert and state your feelings or rights without displaying a lot of anger and intense emotion while doing so.

- **Minimize your demandingness toward self, others, and the world.** Replace the three major musts and absolute shoulds (*"I must ..., she must ..., the world must ..."*) with *preferences, wants, and wishes.* When talking with yourself, about what seems to be angering you, use the words, *"I prefer ..., I want ..., I wish ..."* These words

---

* Chapter Four further explains most of these self-help techniques.

lead to emotional stability. Be aware of what you are telling yourself: about yourself, about others, and about events and situations.

• Acknowledge that situations and events which exist at any given time are bound to happen, given the conditions and forces which are present at that time. Do work to improve those events in the future.

• **Minimize your condemnation & damnation, I-can't-stand-it-itis, and awfulizing (three hot links) and increase your low frustration tolerance (LFT) and low self-acceptance (LSA).**

• **Give up the belief that expressing your anger is healthy.** Anger causes cardiovascular disease and high blood pressure (leading to strokes, etc.). Anger is self-destructive; expressing mild irritation and annoyance can be healthy.

• *Turn your anger down* **rather than expressing it or holding it in.** Expressing your anger is practicing to be angry in the future. Express your annoyance instead. Improve your communication skills and be assertive.

• **When upset, use emotionally cool language when talking with yourself.** Avoid condemnation & damnation self-talk

• **Mentally rehearse what you are going to say and do when facing situations which you anticipate could trigger your anger.**

• **Use coping self-talk statements** such as, *"I don't like it, that's ok, I can stand it anyway."* Count to 10, do it again.

• **Temporarily leave the situation triggering your anger, if possible.** Especially do this if you are highly angry.

- **Use distraction, diversion, and entertainment** by temporarily becoming involved in some pleasurable activity. This helps you to feel less angry in the short run.

- **Avoid becoming depressed or more angry about being angry** (called a secondary emotional problem in Chapter Six). Avoid believing, *"I should not be angry and since I am angry, as I must not be, I'm just worthless and feel even more angry at myself."* Accept and don't condemn yourself if you become angry more often than you wish.

To reduce your upsetness and anger over the long term, also do the following:

- **Consider meeting with a therapist.**

- **Complete the** *Anger And ABCDE Self-Analysis And Improvement Form.* Also, review the *ABC View Of Our Anger.*

- **Keep a Daily Mood Record to better understand your emotions.** Recognize that feelings of anxiety and depression almost always accompany feelings of anger.

- **Detect and identify your irrational beliefs and self-talk** which are mainly responsible for your anger, depression, or anxiety. When searching for irrational beliefs which may be causing your anger, do reconsider your demandingness toward the world, your insistence that others behave a certain way, the three major musts, the five hot links, and the 11 irrational beliefs.

- **Dispute and uproot your irrational beliefs and self-talk causing your anger.** Deepen your conviction in the self-destructiveness of your old irrational beliefs and self-talk causing your anger.

Anger And ABCDE
Self-Analysis And Improvement Form

Date:

A <u>Activating Event</u> (Unpleasant event, situation, or wrongful behavior of others; these can be anticipated events):

B <u>Beliefs</u> And Self-Talk Statements (Your irrational beliefs and self-talk statements; especially your musts, absolute shoulds, and five hot links):

C <u>Consequences:</u> Emotional & Behavioral (Your unpleasant emotion and maladaptive behavior):
Emotions:

Behavior (or contemplated behavior):

D <u>Dispute And Debate</u> (Dispute your irrational beliefs and self-talk; especially your musts, absolute shoulds, and five hot links):

E <u>Effects</u> (Effects Of Dispute: New emotions and behaviors):

Copy this form. Complete the steps in the order of A, C, B, D, and E. When wanting to reduce your anger, follow the self-help methods in Chapters 4 and 5. As you complete B, look for your musts, absolute shoulds, hot links, the 11 irrational beliefs described in Chapter Six.

> # Daily Mood Record:
> ## Record Of Anxiety, Anger, And Depression
>
> On a scale from 1 to 10 write in a number corresponding to your estimated average mood for the day. Mild is 1 to 3, moderate is 4 to 5, high is 6 to 8, and severe is 9 to 10.
>
> | Date/ Time | Anxiety | Anger | Depres- sion | Notes |
> |---|---|---|---|---|
> | | | | | |

The following directions describe how to keep a Daily Mood Record.

First, decide which of the basic emotions you are going to log. Pay close attention to those emotions. Record your approximate average mood for the emotions you have decided to track. Do this each day. Enter any notes on the record that might help you to better understand your emotions.

Main Points To Remember:

• Manage your anger or it will manage you and your relationships. You can't control your anger as long as you believe others cause it.

- It's not the situation (the activating event) that angers us, but what we believe and tell ourselves (beliefs and self-talk) about the situation.

- Our demands (our musts, absolute shoulds), that we place on ourselves, on the behavior of others, and on the world, are what primarily upset and anger us.

- Two common sources of our anger are our low frustration tolerance and threats to our self-esteem.

- Three targets of our anger are: self, others, and the world.

- We have three basic choices of what to do with our anger: *Hold it in; Let it out; or Turn it down*. Believing *"It's healthy to express my anger"* is a myth.

- People can use anger and emotional upsetness as an instrument or lever to get what they want. That anger is called instrumental anger.

- Don't get angry, get annoyed! Replace anger and rage (unhealthy emotions) with annoyance or mild irritation (healthier emotions).

- When angry, complete the *Anger And ABCDE Self-Analysis And Improvement Form* to better understand and manage your anger.

ANYONE CAN BECOME ANGRY. THAT IS EASY. BUT TO BE ANGRY WITH THE RIGHT PERSON, TO THE RIGHT DEGREE, AT THE RIGHT TIME, FOR THE RIGHT PURPOSE, AND IN THE RIGHT WAY, THAT IS NOT EASY. ARISTOTLE

Chapter 9

Managing Depression

DEPRESSION CLOUDS OUR THINKING AND FEELING

"I can't see life's problems and challenges very clearly when I'm in this mood."

A depressed mood clouds our thinking and our ability to avoid, manage, and solve problems. Also, it makes us feel miserable. Depression is largely caused by our beliefs and self-talk.

In this chapter we'll consider: the difference between depression as a problem and depression as a disorder. We'll look at types of depressive disorders, causes of depression including significant losses, low self-acceptance (LSA), irrational beliefs, and specific ways to prevent and manage depression.

Depression can be a problem or a disorder. As an unpleasant emotional *problem*, depression is a temporary mood and is not significantly interfering in one's life. However, depression can become a persistent and severe *disorder* which causes significant emotional distress or impairment in family, social, educational, or vocational functioning.

Depression as a disorder, is "... marked especially by sadness, inactivity, difficulty in thinking and concentration, a significant increase or decrease in appetite and time spent sleeping, feelings of dejection and hopelessness, and sometimes suicidal tendencies (Webster, 1996)." Depression also involves "...feelings of sadness, despair, and discouragement ...slowed thinking, decreased pleasure, decreased purposeful physical activity, guilt and hopelessness, and disorders of eating and sleeping" (Psychiatric Glossary 1994).*

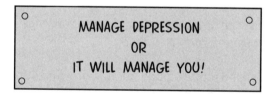

MANAGE DEPRESSION
OR
IT WILL MANAGE YOU!

Depressed individuals usually experience a mixture of anxiety and anger along with their depression. Although unpleasant feelings are primarily those of depression, feelings of anxiety and anger are usually present.

---

* DSM is *The Diagnostic And Statistical Manual Of Mental Disorders, 4th Edition, Text Revision,* 2000 and Psychiatric Glossary is *American Psychiatric Glossary,* 1994 both published by the American Psychiatric Association. Descriptions of depressive disorders for adults are primarily based on these sources.

UNPLEASANT FEELINGS PIE

When experiencing depression, you most certainly feel a measure of anxiety and anger as well. Many individuals are often unaware that they are experiencing one or more of these unpleasant feelings.

Causes of depression include: facing harsh disappointments or a significant loss (losing a job, relationship, spouse, good health); relentlessly *demanding* that a disappointment or loss *must not have occurred*; experiencing various other bad events (unpleasant activating events); and practicing hot, irrational thoughts and self-talk. Depression is also caused by *a negative view of one's self, others, the world, and the future* (Beck & Rush, 1995).

For some people the cause of depression can be partly biological. An imbalance in the chemical transmitters or chemical messengers between neurons in the brain can predispose some people to depression. In bipolar disorder, there is also thought to be an imbalance in brain chemical neurotransmitters. Some medical conditions, such as an underactive thyroid, can produce depressive disorder symptoms. Ask your physician about the need for a physical exam.

To understand and manage depression, use the methods and skills presented in SOS. In order to improve more rapidly, also consider meeting with a therapist.

Talk with your physician or a psychiatrist about antidepressant medication. For some people, medication can be very helpful, especially if the depression is severe. Improved antidepressants are being developed each year. If you begin taking medication, remember that antidepressant medication usually takes two weeks to begin having an effect on depressed mood, so don't give up taking it.

To lessen the pain of depression, many individuals develop drug or alcohol problems. However, trying to soothe depressed feelings with non-prescribed drugs or with alcohol always increases the depression and escalates each of life's problems. Non-prescribed drugs and alcohol also create conflicts with others.

Children and adolescents develop many of the same depressive symptoms as adults. However, children and adolescents are more likely to display irritability and anger along with their depressive symptoms.

Let's look at different types of depressive disorders. As mentioned previously, beware of the "psychology student's disease," believing that you may have most or all of the disorders you're reading about!

TO STRAIGHTEN OUT YOUR EMOTIONS,
FIRST STRAIGHTEN OUT
YOUR BELIEFS AND SELF-TALK.

Early Morning Depression

A Activating Event

"*This is the day I have been dreading.*" (Activating events can be anticipated events.)

Causes

B Beliefs & Self-Talk

"*It's just <u>awful</u> ... <u>I-can't-stand</u> to do it again ... It <u>always</u> happens, week after week ... I <u>shouldn't</u> have to do it! ... Thinking about mowing the grass <u>always</u> makes me so depressed!*"

C Consequences:
Emotional & Behavioral Consequences

"*I'm feeling really discouraged and depressed. I can't get up, I'm too exhausted. But if I stay in bed, it will still be there waiting for me.*"

D Dispute

"*I'm making myself really depressed. I'd prefer not to mow the grass but it <u>isn't</u> <u>awful</u> and <u>I-can-stand-it</u> ... What I tell myself can really influence my mood.*"

Five Kinds Of Depressive Disorders

To meet the criteria for each of the following depressive disorders, an individual needs to experience significant emotional distress or become impaired in family, vocational, educational, or social functioning.

Dysthymic Disorder (dys'•thy'•mic) – significantly depressed mood that continues almost daily for two or more years. An individual can have many of the following symptoms: low self-acceptance (LSA), low self-esteem, feelings of worthlessness and inadequacy, poor concentration, feelings of hopelessness and despair, inappropriate feelings of guilt, self-pity, lowered activity level, loss of interest in pleasurable activities, becoming less talkative, withdrawing from relationships, and exhibiting irritability.
Physical symptoms of dysthymic disorder include: poor appetite or overeating with a change in weight, difficulty sleeping or excessive sleeping, and fatigue.

Major Depressive Disorder – severely depressed mood and symptoms which last two weeks or more. The depressed mood and symptoms are much more severe than for dysthymic disorder. Some unfortunate individuals experience one or more episodes of major depressive disorder in their lifetime.
For major depression, antidepressant medication is usually a helpful and essential part of treatment. Hospitalization is often important or necessary.

Bipolar Disorder (manic-depressive) Bipolar disorder is a severe mood disturbance and includes: manic mood and behavior, depressive mood and behavior, and normal mood and behavior, all of which alternate. The person's mood and behavior may be mostly manic or mostly depressed, but both extremes occur. When manic or depressed, the person is greatly impaired in family, vocational, educational, and social functioning and often needs to be hospitalized for his own safety.

Psychologists and psychiatrists used to call bipolar disorder manic-depressive illness, but no longer do so.

Manic behavior is when a person's mood is greatly elevated and expansive. Any of the following manic symptoms can occur: inflated self-esteem, greatly decreased need for sleep, talkativeness, irritability, racing thoughts, impaired concentration and attention span, greatly increased activity level, increased sexual behavior, foolish behavior, wild spending, and poor judgment. Sometimes the individual develops delusions (false ideas) such as being a great inventor, coming up with a solution to the world's problems, or being persecuted by the CIA.

The person with bipolar disorder experiences depressive mood and behavior as well as manic mood and behavior. When depressed, he feels miserable, hopeless, and despondent. Depressive mood and behavior is similar to that for other depressive disorders. When manic, he usually thinks he is highly productive or creative. However, manic behavior is too self-defeating and disorganized to actually be productive or creative.

To the distress of family members, manic individuals experiencing a pleasant "high" often enjoy their elevated mood, deny they have a problem, and refuse to seek treatment. They become highly irritated if family members press them to get professional help.

Following an episode of bipolar disorder, individuals usually return to their prior behavior and personality. Unfortunately, many people with a history of bipolar disorder have a reoccurrence of this disorder. Medication for bipolar disorder can be very helpful in treating and preventing further occurrences of bipolar disorder.

Superman's Girl Friend
Encounters Bipolar Disorder

Margo Kidder, who played Lois Lane in the popular series of Superman films during the 1980's, reports experiencing repeated episodes of bipolar disorder (manic-depression).*

Margo has experienced mood swings since her teens and has attempted suicide twice. She reports enjoying her "highs," when she feels excited and "all revved up." However, she hates her "lows" and the destructive effects caused by manic-depression on her life and on the life of her daughter.

Once on the way to a speaking engagement in Los Angeles, she developed the idea that the CIA was chasing her and that she *"had to be blown up."* She tried to run away, disguised herself, traded her expensive Armani suit with someone, walked 40 miles, and lived with homeless street people. After being listed as missing for several days, she was found dazed and hiding in the bushes of a stranger's backyard.

Margo received treatment, recovered, and some months later was interviewed on a television news program. She plans to take medication to prevent further bipolar relapses.

Margo Kidder has *accepted* this particular emotional problem without condemning herself and without demanding that it must not be. She states, *"In general, I've been blessed with a wonderful life. Every human being has been given a burden in life, and mine happens to be manic-depression. It is no heavier than anyone else's and it is lighter than many. It is simply the card I drew."*

Cyclothymic Disorder (cy•clo•thy•mic) – a long lasting, fluctuating mood disturbance with many periods of elated and excited mood and many periods of depressed mood.   To receive the diagnosis of cyclothymic disorder,

---

* Margo Kidder was interviewed on the television news program, 20/20.

this fluctuating pattern of mood needs to last for at least two years and to cause the person emotional distress or impairment in family, social, or vocational functioning. Extremes of mood are not as severe as with bipolar disorder (manic-depressive). Others may regard the person as temperamental, moody, unreliable, or unpredictable.

Adjustment Disorder With Depression – following a severely stressful event, situation, or loss (a bad activating event), the individual develops marked depression (extreme feelings of sadness , hopelessness, and guilt; and difficulty concentrating) and becomes impaired in relationships with others or impaired as a student, worker, or homemaker.

Examples of stressful events and losses include marital conflict, divorce, being fired from a job, failing in school, or a bankruptcy. The loss of an important relationship is a common activating event triggering depression. However, one's beliefs and self-talk about the loss or stressful event mainly cause one's depression.

Rates Of Depressive Disorders In Adults

Depressive Disorder	Rates In General Population
Dys•thy•mic Disorder	4% to 8% of Population*
Major Depressive Disorder	12% to 17% of Population*
Bipolar Disorder (Manic-Depressive)**	1% to 2% of Population*
Cy•clo•thy•mic Disorder	Rates are not known
Adjustment Disorder With Depression	Rates are not known

* Rates of a disorder in the general population over one's lifetime. The rates for depression are twice as high for women as for men. Men are more reluctant to seek help, so the rate of depression for men may be underreported.
** Bipolar Disorder was formerly called Manic-Depressive Illness.

---

* Sources are Wilson, G., Nathan, P., O'Leary, K., & Clark, Lee. (1996) and Neal, F., Davison, G., & Haaga, D. (1996).

Losses Often Trigger Depression

LOSS OF A JOB

"When I lost my job, I <u>demanded</u> that it <u>should</u> <u>not</u> <u>have</u> <u>happened</u> and I told myself that I was <u>worthless</u> without it. I have now stopped using destructive self-talk and I no longer feel depressed. I'm interviewing for another job."

LOSS OF A RELATIONSHIP

"I lost my fiancé. For the longest time I <u>demanded</u> that our breakup <u>must</u> <u>not</u> <u>have</u> <u>happened</u>. When I changed my <u>demand</u> that it not happen to a <u>wish</u> that it not happen, I felt more sad than depressed. Now, I can go on."

LOSS OF GOOD HEALTH

"When I lost my good health, I kept <u>demanding</u> that this <u>must</u> <u>not</u> <u>happen</u> to me. I went into a miserable clinical depression. When I <u>stopped</u> <u>demanding</u> that my loss <u>must</u> <u>not</u> <u>happen</u>, I felt much less depressed."

Depression is often triggered by a significant personal loss and our refusal to accept it. One's beliefs and self-talk about the loss cause the depression.

Change your <u>demand</u> that the loss must not have occurred to a <u>preference</u> or <u>wish</u> that it had not occurred. Use these self-talk words with yourself, "<u>wish</u>" and "<u>preference</u>." Your depression will become sadness, a healthier emotion and easier to manage.

Work to change what you can. Ask for serenity to accept what you cannot change.

Losses Can Trigger Depression

There's a difference between sadness, depression, and a lasting depression. *Sadness,* a healthy but unpleasant emotion, is largely caused by believing and telling ourselves that an important loss has occurred. *Depression* is caused by believing a loss has occurred and telling ourselves that the loss *is awful and that it must not have occurred.* A *lasting depression* is caused by continuously telling yourself that the loss must not have occurred, that you will never accept it, that it is awful, and that you can't-stand-it. *Work to change what you can. Ask for serenity to accept what you cannot change.*

How could someone *not* be lastingly affected and depressed by a severe tragedy such as the unexpected death of a child? How we respond to and accept bad events is primarily determined by what we believe and tell ourselves about the bad event. Let's consider what different family members tell themselves about a child's death.

"Daddy shouldn't have backed over him."

Mr. Lyons reached under his truck and removed the body of his four year-old son, after accidentally backing over him. Nineteen year-old Brittany watched as her brother's body was placed on the living room couch.

Mr. and Mrs. Lyons grieved over their son's death and over time, although greatly saddened, accepted it. Brittany, however, refused to accept her brother's death or her father's role in it, saying *it must not have happened.* She obsessed about the accident, endlessly repeating to herself, *"Daddy packed him in over his shoulder and laid him on the couch. ...How could anyone do something so stupid, ... It shouldn't have happened. ...Daddy shouldn't have backed over him."*

After months of continuous, harmful self-talk and steadfastly refusing to accept his death, Brittany became mute and remained nearly motionless. She went into a state of stupor and was hospitalized.

People have different beliefs and self-talk about a personal tragedy and accepting it or not accepting it. These beliefs and self-talk can be rational and self-helping or irrational and self-downing. Our beliefs and self-talk determine the feelings that follow. Brittany constantly reindoctrinated herself with, *"It shouldn't have happened. I can't accept it."* Of the 11 irrational beliefs, the ones most influencing Brittany are the following:

#9.   **My past history mainly causes my present feelings and behavior; things from my past which once strongly influenced me will always strongly influence me.**

#3.   **The world must be fair. People must act fairly and considerately and if they don't, they are bad, wicked, villainous, or incredibly stupid; they should be severely blamed and punished.**

#5.   **There isn't much I can do about my anxiety, anger, depression, or unhappiness because my feelings are caused by what happens to me.** (The remaining *eleven irrational beliefs* are described in Chapter Six.)

Unlike her parents, Brittany blocked the healing power of *the passage of time.* She did this by refusing to accept painful reality and constantly reindoctrinating herself with, *"It shouldn't have happened. I can't accept it."*

Rational emotive behavior therapy, the basis of SOS, is useful in helping individuals adjust to tragic events. The emotional support of family and friends also is important, however. Brittany received therapy and after a year was considerably improved.

TO BELIEVE,
"MY FEELINGS ARE MAINLY CAUSED
BY WHAT HAPPENS TO ME,"
IS A RECIPE FOR DEPRESSION.

Accepting A Severe Loss

The challenge for someone experiencing a severe loss is to find some way to accept it without continuously demanding that *it must not have occurred*. Let's see how two people tried to accept their losses.

"What would my son say to me?"

This was the second time a burglar had entered Ralph's home at night, but this time he was prepared. Ralph had purchased a handgun to protect his home and family.

Ralph heard a noise downstairs. He grabbed the gun and rushed across the hall to Christopher's room to see if his young son was safe. At the same time, Christopher burst out of his room. Christopher's door hit the gun, causing it to discharge. One bullet entered Christopher's head. He died in his father's arms.

Ralph entered treatment for posttraumatic stress disorder and to come to terms with the grief and guilt he felt.

After months of therapy and continued inability to accept his loss and forgive himself, Ralph's therapist asked, *"If Christopher could briefly come back to you, what do you think he would say?"* After weeks of thinking about this question, Ralph said he thought that his son would say something like, *"Dad, forgive yourself, accept this, and be with Momma."*

Ralph worked on believing this "advice from his son." With this advice to accept his loss, and with the passage of time, Ralph's deep depression began lifting.

GOD GRANT ME
SERENITY TO ACCEPT THE THINGS I CANNOT CHANGE,
COURAGE TO CHANGE THE THINGS I CAN,
AND
WISDOM TO KNOW THE DIFFERENCE.

"Will this loss ruin the rest of my life?"

Dana, a middle-aged wife and mother, returned home from her job as a bank clerk and learned that her husband had just died. Dana loved him and they had a satisfying marriage. After a year of struggling with grief and loneliness, she achieved a new way of thinking about her loss in order to help end her depression.

She finally arrived at the belief, and frequently repeated it to herself, *"I have two choices. I can accept my loss as irreversible reality and go on with my life. Or, I can* not *accept my loss and let it ruin the rest of my life."*

Frequently repeating these self-talk statements helped Dana to accept her loss, become much less depressed, and indeed go on with her life.

Depression And ABC View Of Our Emotions

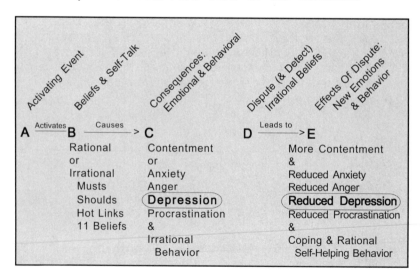

Replace Low Self-Acceptance (LSA) And Low Self-Esteem With Self-Acceptance

NO LOW SELF-ACCEPTANCE

LSA, for many, is based on the irrational belief –
"I must be loved and approved of by all others."

A helpful coping or dispute statement is – *" I don't have to be loved or approved by all others to accept myself."*

Self-esteem is self-respect, self-worth, confidence, and satisfaction in oneself. *Base your self-esteem on steadfast acceptance of yourself* and not on how much you value your personal characteristics or accomplishments or being loved or approved by all others.* "Realize that true self-respect never comes from the approval of others but from liking yourself …" (Ellis, 1994, p. 108).

Attempting to increase your self-esteem sounds like a healthy goal. However, if you pursue the goal of increased self-esteem by improving your personal characteristics and accomplishments, or by seeking the approval of more people, you could escalate your depression and lower your self-esteem (Borcherdt, 1989).

---

* Distinguish between (1) rating your accomplishments (healthy) and (2) rating yourself as a person based on your accomplishments (unhealthy).

PRACTICING LOW SELF-ACCEPTANCE (LSA)
& LOW SELF-ESTEEM SELF-TALK STATEMENTS

"*§æ!±»! I missed again! That is pitiful! I'm worthless
if I don't get off a good serve this time as I absolutely
must do. Saying that to myself will really make me
try hard. Of course, if I miss this serve I will feel like
a worthless *§æ!±»! I'm not playing as well as I used
to. Maybe tennis isn't my sport."

This self-talk causes low self-acceptance (LSA) and
low self-esteem. It's important to use rational rather
than irrational self-talk statements to motivate
yourself. This tennis player has linked I must with
I'm worthless and continues to rehearse negative
self-talk statements. Don't label yourself with *§æ!±»!
labels!

Some unfortunate people believe that self-
improvement is more likely to result from self-
condemnation than self-acceptance.

Although self-esteem and self-acceptance are similar
terms, I prefer self-acceptance. Self-acceptance is the
steadfast acceptance of self and refusal to give an overall,

global rating such as "worthless" or "perfect" to yourself (Dryden & Neenan, 1994). Don't label yourself! Rate what you do, but don't rate yourself as a person; there's a difference. A self-accepting person believes, *"I steadfastly accept myself as a person, although I may not like all of my behaviors and actions. I am willing to rate, evaluate, and work to improve my actions and behaviors."*

Low self-acceptance (LSA) can result from insisting on love and approval by all others because almost no one can expect to get this. LSA can also result from assigning yourself a poor, overall global rating based on personal characteristics, actions, or accomplishments.

Feelings of guilt, as when we break our own moral code, can cause LSA. Replace feelings of guilt with regret (described in Chapter Four) and resolve to improve your future behavior.

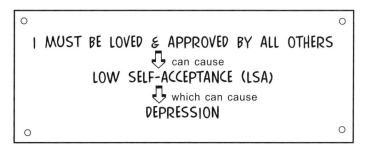

I MUST BE LOVED & APPROVED BY ALL OTHERS
⬇ can cause
LOW SELF-ACCEPTANCE (LSA)
⬇ which can cause
DEPRESSION

Self-acceptance leads to more contentment, increased success in meeting goals, and to reduced anxiety, anger, and depression. Accepting yourself makes it easier to accept others, although you may not always like the way they behave. Self-acceptance is important in motivating ourselves to achieve our goals and in managing our relationships with others. *Managing relationships* and *motivating ourselves to achieve our goals* are both important components of emotional intelligence as described in Chapter One.

Strive for self-acceptance <u>and</u> work toward self-improvement. But don't base your self-acceptance on your personal characteristics, your achievements, or on being loved or approved by others. Achievements, success, and being loved or approved by others can fade, leaving you to cope with low self-acceptance and consequently with depression, anxiety, or anger.

Avoid self-downing statements and using the hot link of *I'm worthless*. When greatly disappointing yourself, don't get into the habit of also *condemning and damning* yourself (turning the hot link of *condemnation and damnation* on yourself). These irrational self-talk statements lead to depression and guilt (Nottingham, 1994).

When feeling worthless, strive to believe a rational alternative belief. It is, *"I'm not a perfect person. I'm fallible with strengths and weaknesses just as other people. I will try not to further upset myself about my upsetness."*

Many individuals who suffer from depression and low self-acceptance stumble into a pattern of irrational beliefs and self-talk which lead to self-hate. Is the basic problem that these individuals need to improve themselves or learn to accept themselves? The answer is – *work on steadfastly accepting yourself.*

Avoid low self-acceptance (LSA) which is a core cause of depression, social phobia (also called social anxiety disorder), some eating disorders, some anger problems, and other disorders.

Of the 11 irrational beliefs which contribute to low self-acceptance (and which need to be uprooted), the following are most significant:

#1.   **It is a dire necessity for me to be loved or approved by almost all others, who are significant to me.**

#2.   **I must be thoroughly competent, adequate, and achieving, in all important respects, in order to be worthwhile.**

#5.   **There isn't much I can do about my low self-acceptance or low self-esteem, because my self-acceptance and self-esteem are caused by what happens to me, how others rate me, and how they treat me.** (This irrational belief is slightly modified from the original #5 irrational belief in Chapter Six.)

BURDENED BY DEPRESSION
AND
"BEING DEPRESSED ABOUT BEING DEPRESSED"

*"*This §æ!±»! depression is really a burden and
<u>I-can't-stand-it</u>. I <u>must</u> <u>not</u> <u>be</u> <u>depressed</u> and since
I am, as I must not be, I'm just <u>worthless</u>."*

*Becoming further depressed about being depressed
is a secondary (additional) emotional problem* which
intensifies one's total burden of unhappiness and
distress. For more cautions regarding *"being upset
about being upset"* see "Avoiding Secondary
Emotional Problems" in Chapter Six.

Self-Help For Depression

When you are feeling discouraged and depressed,
review the following checklist of causes and help for
depression. Chapter Four discusses many of these
methods. Practice the following to interrupt and manage
your feelings of depression.

- **Acknowledge that your beliefs and self-talk
  mainly cause your emotions** rather than actual
  events, losses, or practical problems (that is,
  activating events).

- **Deal first with your emotional problem** (your upsetness and depression) before attempting to deal with your practical problem or loss (the activating event that seems to be depressing you).

- **Replace unhealthy emotions with healthy ones.** Replace depression (an unhealthy emotion) with sadness (a more healthy emotion). Replace anger with annoyance.

- **Replace the three major musts and absolute shoulds** (*"I must ..., she must ..., the world must ..."*) with *preferences, wants, and wishes*. When talking with yourself, about what seems to be depressing you, use the words, *"I prefer ..., I want ..., I wish ..."* Be aware of what you are telling yourself about yourself, about others, and about events and situations.

- **Drop any of the five hot links** (condemnation & damnation, I-can't-stand-it-itis, awfulizing, I'm worthless, and always & never) that you are using. A global self-evaluation, *"I'm worthless,"* needs to be challenged and discarded.

- **Use emotionally cool language when talking with yourself**.

- When confronted with frustrations and losses, **repeat coping self-talk statements** such as, *"I don't like it, that's ok, I can stand it anyway."*

- **Use distraction, diversion, and entertainment** by temporarily becoming involved in some pleasurable activity.

- **Avoid becoming depressed about your depression** (called a secondary emotional problem in Chapter Six). Avoid believing, *"I should not be depressed and since I am depressed, as I must not be, I'm just worthless and feel even more depressed..."*

- **Replace low self-acceptance (LSA) and low self-esteem with steadfast self-acceptance.** Do evaluate and work to improve your behavior and actions, but don't give yourself a global overall evaluation.

- **Consider obtaining a physical examination, a trial period on antidepressant medication, and meeting with a therapist.**

To reduce your depression over the long term, also do the following:

- **When feeling depressed, complete the Depression And ABCDE Self-Analysis And Improvement Form.**

- **Keep a Daily Mood Record to better understand your emotions.** Recognize that feelings of anxiety and anger almost always accompany feelings of depression.

- **Detect and identify your irrational beliefs and self-talk** which are largely responsible for your depression, low self-acceptance, feelings of worthlessness, or the deepening of your feelings of loss. When searching for irrational beliefs which may be causing your depression, also review the *eleven irrational beliefs* in Chapter Six.

- **Dispute and uproot your irrational beliefs and self-talk causing depression, low self-acceptance, feelings of worthlessness, and the insistence that your losses "must not have occurred."** Deepen your conviction in the self-destructiveness of your old, irrational beliefs and self-talk.

Depression And ABCDE
Self-Analysis And Improvement Form

Date:

A <u>Activating</u> <u>Event</u> (Unpleasant event, situation, or loss; these can be anticipated events or losses):

B <u>Beliefs</u> **And Self-Talk Statements** (Your irrational beliefs and self-talk statements; especially your musts, absolute shoulds, and five hot links):

C <u>Consequences:</u> **Emotional & Behavioral** (Your unpleasant emotion and maladaptive behavior):
Emotions:

Behavior (or contemplated behavior):

D <u>Dispute And Debate</u> (Dispute your irrational beliefs and self-talk; especially your musts, absolute shoulds, and five hot links):

E <u>Effects</u> (Effects Of Dispute: New emotions and behaviors):

Copy this form. Complete the steps in the order of A, C, B, D, and E. When depressed, follow the self-help methods in Chapters 4 and 5. As you complete B, look for your musts, shoulds, hot links, and the 11 irrational beliefs in Chapter Six.

```
┌─────────────────────────────────────────────────────────┐
│                    Daily Mood Record:                     │
│        Record Of Anxiety, Anger, And Depression           │
├───────────────────────────────────────────────────────────┤
│     On a scale from 1 to 10 write in a number corresponding│
│  to your estimated average mood for the day.  Mild is 1 to 3,│
│  moderate is 4 to 5, high is 6 to 8, and severe is 9 to 10.│
├────────┬────────┬───────┬─────────┬────────────────────────┤
│ Date/  │ Anxiety│ Anger │ Depres- │         Notes          │
│ Time   │        │       │ sion    │                        │
│        │        │       │         │                        │
│        │        │       │         │                        │
│        │        │       │         │                        │
└────────┴────────┴───────┴─────────┴────────────────────────┘
```

The following directions describe how to keep a Daily Mood Record.

First, decide which of the basic emotions you are going to log. Pay close attention to those emotions. Record your approximate average mood for the emotions you have decided to track. Do this each day. Enter any notes on the record that might help you to better understand your emotions.

Main Points To Remember:

• A depressed mood causes distress and clouds our thinking and our ability to avoid, manage, and solve problems.

- Causes of depression include: harsh disappointments or significant losses; our relentless *demands* that a disappointment or loss *must not have occurred*; irrational beliefs and self-talk; and for some people, biological factors.

- Depression can become more than a problem; it can become a persistent and severe disorder.

- Replace low self-acceptance (LSA) and low self-esteem with steadfast self-acceptance. Do evaluate and work to improve your behavior and actions, however.

- Complete the *Depression And ABCDE Self-Analysis And Improvement Form* to better understand and manage your depression.

- If you are significantly and persistently depressed, talk with your physician or a psychiatrist about possible physical causes of your depression and a trial period on antidepressant medication.

- Use a number of additional SOS self-help methods to deal with your depressed feelings.

- Test your understanding of Chapters Seven, Eight, and Nine. Turn to Chapter 12 and complete Part Three of the quizzes and exercises.

Part Four

HELPING OURSELVES IN MORE WAYS

Chapter 10

Coping With Difficult People

TWO DIFFICULT PEOPLE

In this chapter we'll consider:

- the importance of first managing our emotions and then dealing with difficult people

- common beliefs and self-talk causing us to feel upset and angry when we are around difficult people

- guessing at the irrational beliefs of *your* difficult person

- recommendations for dealing with difficult people

"Phil Is <u>Our</u> SOB"

Jacob stopped in his supervisor's office to complain about Phil, well-known to co-workers as a troublemaker and difficult person. After listening to a list of complaints, his supervisor replied, *"Every organization has it's SOB! Phil is <u>our</u> SOB. You'll have to adjust!"*

Jacob left his supervisor's office annoyed, but acknowledging that he would need to adjust his thinking and emotions. He actually had suspected that this would be the case before complaining.

First Deal With Your Distress, Then With The Difficult Person

Difficult people may impede our goals, threaten our self-esteem and self-acceptance, act in arrogant and annoying ways, frustrate us, and use unpleasant methods to control situations *and us*. Robert Bramson, in his book *Coping With Difficult People*, labels these people as, "tanks, snipers, exploders, bulldozers, wet blankets, silent clams, complainers, procrastinators, and know-it-alls" (1981).

To cope with difficult people, manage your emotional reaction to them <u>first</u>. There are two reasons why we should manage our emotions before dealing with a difficult person. It's more comfortable to relate to others without feeling a lot of anxiety, anger, intense frustration, or having our self-esteem and self-acceptance threatened. Also, we can think more clearly and behave more effectively when dealing with difficult people if we are not severely emotionally upset with them.

Dealing With Difficult People, an audiotape lecture by Albert Ellis (1991), is available from Albert Ellis Institute For Rational Emotive Behavior Therapy.

Our emotions and behavior result mainly from our beliefs and self-talk, rather than from the actual events and people in our lives. *It's not unpleasant people, who cause our distress, but rather our beliefs and self-talk about them and their behavior.* We are responsible for creating our own emotions. If difficult-acting people upset us, we have given them permission to do so. The familiar illustration, *ABC View Of Our Emotions*, shows how we upset ourselves when we encounter difficult people.

ABC View Of Our Emotions

A ——Activates/Triggers—— B ——Causes——> C
Activating Event   Beliefs & Self-Talk   Consequences: Emotional & Behavioral
Actions of a   **Anxiety, Anger**
difficult person   **Heightened frustration**
Low self-acceptance

Chapter Four introduced the importance of dealing with *our emotional problem before our practical problem.* The behavior of a difficult person is *our practical problem*, and that behavior is also called an A activating event. Our B beliefs and self-talk about the actions of a difficult person largely cause our C, consequences of anxiety, anger, heightened frustration, or low self-acceptance (LSA).

An Angry Husband

The husband of one of my college students burst into my office, angry about his wife's grade on one of my psychology exams. He came to see me about his wife's grade even though she is an ardent feminist. Because she had missed taking the test when it was scheduled, I deducted three points from her test score, as I customarily do when students miss exams. I thought three out of 60 points was a rather minor penalty for taking the exam late.

However, her husband was irate, demanded that her score be changed, and told me that any penalty was unfair. His anger and insistence that her score be changed was *my practical problem*. Before I dealt with *my practical problem*, I first had to deal with *my emotional problem* – my anger over what I judged to be a heavy-handed, absurd demand to change her grade. After I calmed myself, I more effectively dealt with him.

Common B Beliefs And Self-Talk Causing Us To Become Upset Around Difficult People

What do we tell ourselves that disturbs us so much when we are around troublemakers and other difficult people? Let's look at irrational beliefs which cause us to become unduly upset with a difficult person.

We all experience frustration in dealing with others. *Frustration with others is not getting what you want from them.* Low frustration tolerance (LFT) results from believing, *"Others absolutely must give me what I want and behave as I want, and if they don't, it's awful and I-can't-stand-it."*

Work on increasing your LFT, something over which *you* have considerable control. Changing the other person is something over which you usually have little or no control.

What causes low frustration tolerance and how do you improve your LFT so you feel less distressed? To detect your beliefs which cause low frustration tolerance, ask yourself, *"What am I saying to myself about this person? What am I telling myself about his or her actions? What am I insisting or demanding that this person do or stop doing?"*

A DIFFICULT PERSON

"My office door is always open. See me anytime you want! You're always welcome."

Difficult people often give confusing, contradictory messages.

When you feel extremely frustrated or upset with others, silently repeat coping self-talk statements to yourself. Repeating these statements will help to increase your ability to tolerate the frustration. The following are examples of coping statements:

"I dislike this person's behavior, but I can stand it."

"Sometimes relationships are frustrating, but I can stand the frustration."

"Life is tough, but I can take it."

"Human behavior is absurd."

"I don't like it, that's ok, I can stand it anyway."

What other irrational beliefs contribute to our low frustration tolerance and distress when we relate to difficult people? The most likely culprits are: the *three major musts* (especially the second major must – *he or she must...*), *absolute shoulds*, and *five hot connecting links* (condemnation & damnation, I-can't-stand-it-itis, awfulizing, I'm worthless, and always & never).

Demanding that someone change, and telling ourselves that if he doesn't change, *it's awful, I-can't-stand-it, he should be damned* (or other hot links) causes us to be emotionally upset. Merely desiring, wanting, and preferring that someone change leads to less distress.

As you look for irrational beliefs causing you to become unduly upset with difficult people, review the *eleven common irrational beliefs causing emotional distress*, first presented in Chapter Six. Of the six common irrational beliefs listed below, #3 is the most influential.

#1.   **It is a dire necessity for me to be loved or approved by almost all others, who are significant to me.**
If this difficult person does not approve of me as he must, it's awful, I-can't-stand-it, I'm worthless, he should be damned. I'm an RP (rotten person) and no good.

#2.   **I must be thoroughly competent, adequate, and achieving, in all important respects, in order to be worthwhile.**
I must be 100% competent and if this difficult person threatens my feelings of competence and my self-acceptance, it's awful, I-can't-stand-it, I'm worthless, she should be damned.

#3.   **The world must be fair. People must act fairly and considerately and if they don't, they are bad, wicked, villainous, or incredibly stupid; they should be severely blamed and punished.**
And if the difficult people in my life don't act fairly and reasonably, as they must, it's awful, I-can't-stand-it, I'm worthless, and they should be condemned and punished.

#5. **There isn't much I can do about my anxiety, anger, depression, or unhappiness because my feelings are caused by what happens to me** *(and how people treat me)*.
Difficult people must treat me well and if they don't, I can't help feeling anxious, angry, or depressed.

#8. **I'm quite dependent on others and need someone stronger than myself to rely upon; I cannot run my own life.**
I must have someone to depend upon and that person must treat me well. If he doesn't treat me well, as he must, then it's awful, I-can't-stand-it, I'm worthless.

#10. **I must become very anxious, angry, or depressed over someone else's problems and disturbances, if I care about that person**.
Others whom I care about must not be significantly troubled and miserable and if they are, as they absolutely must not be, it's awful, I-can't-stand-it, I'm worthless, and it will always be this way. I must not be happy knowing that others are miserable.

Look in Chapter Six for *rational alternative beliefs* which can replace the above irrational beliefs. Work on uprooting your irrational beliefs and adopting rational alternative beliefs so that difficult people "won't drive you crazy."

Continue disputing and challenging your irrational beliefs until you can stand the behavior of difficult people. Prior chapters, and especially Chapters Three and Four, teach how to dispute and uproot your irrational beliefs.

When relating to a difficult person, turn your demand that she change her behavior into a preference that she change her behavior. Acknowledge to yourself your preference that she change her behavior, but that it's not essential for your happiness or survival.

> FIRST DEAL WITH OUR OWN DISTRESS,
> THEN WITH THE DIFFICULT PERSON

A DIFFICULT PERSON

"Since we just met, I'd like to mention that I have 'Intermittent Explosive Disorder.' It's a recognized 'psychiatric DSM impulse-control disorder,' where a person has unexpected episodes of aggression. But I'm working on controlling it."

*"My ex-friends think it's a bigger problem than it is! But they always make too much out of things. Now, let's get better acquainted."**

A Difficult Boss

Ed enjoyed his job as a successful, well-paid, pharmaceutical sales representative in spite of Mr. Bratcher, his sales manager.

Mr. Bratcher reduced the territory of his sales reps and then increased their sales quotas. He frequently sent out hostile and demanding voice mail, faxes, e-mail, memos, and letters to his reps,

---

* Intermittent Explosive Disorder is an Impulse-Control Disorder characterized by unexpected and specific "episodes of failure to resist aggressive impulses resulting in serious assaults or destruction of property." It is coded 312.34 in *The Diagnostic And Statistical Manual Of Mental Disorders, 4th Edition, Text Revision, 2000,* published by the American Psychiatric Association.

threatening them with their jobs if they didn't increase sales. In face-to-face contacts, Mr. Bratcher alternated between threatening his staff and acting friendly.

Ed avoided upsetting himself about Mr. Bratcher by disputing his own irrational beliefs and engaging in rational self-talk. Ed would think to himself, *"I enjoy my job, it pays well, and the only drawback is my boss. I don't like him, and I wish they would fire him, but I can stand him. I'm not going to upset myself by demanding that he change his behavior or treat me fairly. This isn't a perfect world, and I'm not going to frustrate myself by demanding that it be perfect."*

DEMANDING THAT OTHERS CHANGE
CAUSES EMOTIONAL DISTRESS.
PREFERRING THAT OTHERS CHANGE
LEADS TO CALMNESS

Guess At The Irrational Beliefs Of Your Difficult Person

The next time you become bored during a dull class or meeting, think of your difficult person, and analyze his ABC's. Guess at his irrational beliefs and self-talk.

The situation that triggers his upsetness with you or someone else is his *A activating event*. His *C consequences* are the emotions and behaviors which he displays during and after the unpleasant situation.

Next is the challenging part. What do you think are the *B's* (the *irrational beliefs and self-talk),* which cause him to act controlling, belligerent, or angry? What is he likely to be saying to himself about another person? What is he insisting or demanding that this other person do or stop doing? Consider the *three major musts* and the *five hot connecting links.* Also, remember the *eleven common irrational beliefs causing emotional distress.*

ABC's Of An Angry Husband

Let's analyze the ABC's of "the angry husband" who burst into my office.

His *A activating event* was probably his wife telling him about the three-point penalty she received for taking my exam late. An important part of his activating event was undoubtedly his observation of her frustration, distress, or anger about receiving the penalty.

The *C consequences, emotional and behavioral*, were clearly evident. He was angry, burst into my office, and demanded that I drop the three-point penalty on his wife's exam.

His *B beliefs and self-talk* probably included: *"My wife absolutely must not be upset by this unreasonable professor, and she must not be penalized for her late exam! If she is upset, as she must not be, it's HTA (horrible, terrible, awful), I can't-stand-it, and he should be damned! What kind of husband would put up with such an awful injustice to his wife?"*

Methods For Coping
With Difficult People

Don't quit a job, attempt to handle a bad situation, or end a troubled relationship while you are significantly emotionally distressed. After managing your low frustration tolerance and anger, decide on a realistic goal regarding your relationship with your difficult person. Next, determine a plan for the best course of action.

After long consideration, you may decide it's best to terminate your relationship with a person. However, if you allow *only your emotions* to control your behavior, you may find that your only accomplishments were releasing anger, expressing rage, or seeking revenge. And anyone can do those things!

It's best to change your anger to annoyance. Then, if you do express annoyance, try to express it with the right person, to the right degree, at the right time, for the right purpose, and in the right way. Not doing so may damage a relationship that you want to continue in the future. If you express intense anger or rage, you may defeat *yourself* as well as the person troubling you. Also, expressing anger at most people, merely convinces them of the correctness of their foolish, obnoxious behavior.

Expressing intense anger is a poor method for getting a person to change her behavior. Getting angry and threatening to spank may cause your daughter to straighten her cluttered room this afternoon. However, her room will probably be cluttered again tomorrow. There are more effective methods for getting her to change her behavior.

The following are specific methods for coping with difficult people.

- Acknowledge that it's not unpleasant people, but rather our beliefs about them and their behavior, which primarily cause our distress.

- To cope with difficult people, first manage your emotional reaction to them.

- Focus on changing your feelings of anger to less intense feelings of annoyance, displeasure, or disappointment.

- Express your annoyance and displeasure, but not intense anger. You don't have to become angry first before expressing your annoyance.

- Be assertive, rather than passive or aggressive, in stating what you want.*

- Negotiate with your difficult person and be willing to compromise.

- Walk out of the room and separate until both of you have calmed down. As you leave, say something like, "We need a break from this discussion."

---

* *Your Perfect Right* (2001), by Alberti & Emmons, helps individuals to stand up for their rights and to manage interpersonal problems with appropriate assertiveness. Chapter 12 also describes this book.

- Accept your difficult person but not his behavior. People are fallible and your difficult person is no exception.

- Forgive the person for his foolish, unreasonable, and illogical behavior.

- Complete the Difficult People And ABCDE Self-Analysis And Improvement Form.

- Try to see the other person's point of view. Ask enough questions until you can accurately repeat and summarize her viewpoint. Be able to paraphrase her position so that she agrees that you have accurately stated it.* Accurately stating another person's position doesn't mean that you accept it, merely that you understand it. Feeling they are understood, others will often become a little more reasonable.

- Leave the situation and become involved in a pleasant activity.

- Review again, this list of SOS methods for dealing with difficult people.

- Accept what you can't change.

```
┌─────────────────────────────────────────┐
│ ○                                      ○ │
│     YOU CAN'T MANAGE RELATIONSHIPS       │
│                  UNTIL                    │
│        YOU MANAGE YOUR EMOTIONS          │
│ ○                                      ○ │
└─────────────────────────────────────────┘
```

---

* *People Skills* (1979), by Bolton, teaches negotiation, conflict-resolution, assertiveness, and listening skills. Chapter 12 describes this book.

Difficult People And ABCDE
Self-Analysis And Improvement Form

Date:

A <u>Activating Event</u> (Unpleasant event, situation, or wrongful behavior of a difficult person; these can be anticipated events):

B <u>Beliefs</u> And Self-Talk Statements (Your irrational beliefs and self-talk statements; especially your musts, absolute shoulds, and five hot links):

C <u>Consequences:</u> Emotional & Behavioral (Your unpleasant emotion and maladaptive behavior):
Emotions:

Behavior (or contemplated behavior):

D <u>Dispute And Debate</u> (Dispute your irrational beliefs and self-talk; especially your musts, absolute shoulds, and five hot links):

E <u>Effects</u> (Effects Of Dispute: New emotions and behaviors):

Copy this form. Complete the steps in the order of A, C, B, D, and E. When wanting to reduce your low frustration tolerance and anger, follow the self-help methods in Chapters 4 and 5. As you complete B, look for your musts, absolute shoulds, hot links, and the 11 irrational beliefs described in Chapter Six.

Coping With The Difficult Child

CHILD REARING *MISTAKES* WHICH PARENTS MAKE

You are a role model for your child!

Model only behavior that you want to see your child demonstrate.

Parents constantly demonstrate or "model" behavior which their children observe. *Your child learns how to behave and manage her emotions by observing and imitating your behavior and the behavior of others.* Don't unintentionally demonstrate behavior that you wouldn't want to later see in your child. A major cause of problem behavior in young children is children observing and imitating the unacceptable behavior of others.

Your daughter pays particularly close attention to you when you are frustrated with a problem or having a conflict with another person. *By watching you, she is learning how she might handle her own emotions, frustrations, and conflicts with others, in the future.*

> MANAGE YOUR EMOTIONS.
> BE A GOOD ROLE MODEL
> FOR YOUR CHILD!

If you use a lot of sarcasm and criticism in dealing with family members or other people, you're actually teaching your child to use back-talk and complaining as a way of dealing with you and other people. By watching their parents, some kids learn that people swear if they get hurt. Sometimes, children learn to have temper tantrums by watching their parents lose control, or threaten to lose control of their emotions and behavior. *You are a role model for your child whether you want to be or not! Be a good model!*

In my experience, another major cause of problem behavior in young children is parents accidentally rewarding bad behavior. Remember the example of Michael (on page 179) who used emotional upsetness and anger to force a Coke from his mother. Mother couldn't stand his belligerent, demanding behavior and, consequently, gave him what he was demanding. When Michael wants something else from his mother in the future, what kind of behavior do you think he will use to get it? Rewarding problem behavior strengthens it and causes future problems for both parent and child.

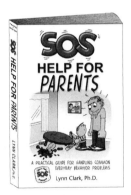

The *SOS Help For Parents* program teaches over 20 methods and skills for helping to improve the problem behavior of young children.*

The Video SOS Help For Parents is a behavior management and parent education program used by counselors and educators and in many college classes. Video clips in English and Spanish may be viewed at the SOS website, <http://www.sosprograms.com>

All of the child management methods presented in the *SOS Help For Parents* book and video-based education program can be used by teachers, as well as parents.

Withhold the object or activity (such as a cookie before supper) your child is trying to force from you. It's acceptable to give your son a cookie before dinner but not if he is using bad behavior to force one from you.

If your child is between the ages of two and twelve, you can use a number of methods for improving her behavior and emotional adjustment. Consider helping your child using methods from *SOS Help For Parents*, a book and program which I developed for parents of children between two and twelve.

MANAGE YOUR CHILDREN
BEFORE THEY MANAGE YOU!

Improving your parenting skills will improve your child's behavior and will help your relationship. Parents have considerable ability to improve the behavior of young children, even hard-to-manage children. *Don't wait until your child is an adolescent to improve your parenting skills!*

Help your child to improve his emotional intelligence, including his ability to manage his feelings. Since emotional intelligence is learned rather than inherited, it can be improved. As he grows older, his success in attaining goals, happiness, and freedom from emotional problems will be highly dependent upon his emotional intelligence.

Five Abilities Of Emotional Intelligence

- Knowing our emotions
- Managing our emotions
- Recognizing emotions in others
- Managing relationships with others
- Motivating ourselves to achieve our goals

Help your daughter learn to listen to her self-talk. Begin teaching her the ABC's of Emotions and continue until she is old enough to leave home. Start at a level appropriate for her age. If she is young, consider demonstrating the ABC's with ABC building blocks.

In a nutshell, A's are the bad events. B's are our self-talk, what we tell ourselves about those bad events. C's are our feelings and behaviors. Our self-talk strongly controls our feelings. You need to pay close attention and listen carefully, to learn what your self-talk is saying.

Main Points To Remember:

- It's not unpleasant people, who cause our distress, but primarily our beliefs and self-talk about them and their actions.

- The behavior of a difficult person is our A activating event. Our B's are our beliefs and self-talk about the actions of a difficult person. Our B's largely cause our C's, consequences of anxiety, anger, or heightened frustration.

- To cope with difficult people, first manage your emotional reaction to them.

- Look for your own irrational beliefs causing you to become unduly upset with difficult people.

- Demanding that someone change, and telling ourselves that if he doesn't change, *it's awful, I-can't-stand-it, and he should be damned*, causes us to be emotionally upset and less effective when relating to him.

- When upset with difficult people, complete the *Difficult People And ABCDE Self-Analysis And Improvement Form* to better understand and manage your feelings.

Main Points To Remember when helping children to become better adjusted in their behavior and emotions:

- Be a good role model for your child, especially when you are upset or in a conflict with another person. He is learning how to manage frustration, disappointment, anger, and conflict by observing you.

- Don't accidentally reward bad behavior. Behavior which is rewarded is strengthened and is more likely to occur in the future.

- Help your child to improve her emotional intelligence. Begin to teach her the ABC's of her emotions and how her self-talk is a major cause of her emotions and behavior.

- *SOS Help For Parents* is for parents (and others) who help children two to twelve years old. Use this book to improve your child's behavior and emotional adjustment.

IT'S EASIER TO IMPROVE A CHILD'S BEHAVIOR
THAN A PARENT'S BEHAVIOR!

DON'T WAIT UNTIL YOUR CHILD'S ADOLESCENCE
TO IMPROVE YOUR PARENTING SKILLS!

Chapter 11

More Ways To Help Ourselves

DEAL WITH THE WORLD AS IT IS,
NOT AS IT "MUST BE" OR "SHOULD BE"

"We have both agreed that our boat <u>should not be leaking</u> and have condemned and damned it! We have also agreed that <u>the world should be fair</u> and that we <u>shouldn't have to deal</u> with this problem! Now what are we going to do?"

It's more adaptive to accept unpleasant reality and quickly deal with it than shoulding, musting, and demanding that it not be.

In this chapter we'll learn more ways to help ourselves. It's important and self-helping to:

• Avoid procrastination and perfectionism

• Study and repeatedly practice the many self-help methods presented in SOS.

• Accept the fact that there will be periods of time when we'll have reduced ability to manage our emotions

• Know about additional self-help resources, and

• Understand when and how to get professional help

Avoid Procrastination

Procrastination is putting off, delaying, and avoiding certain actions. People procrastinate on many things: preparing their income tax, writing a term paper, and doing chores. Often, such procrastination results in additional problems.

As we go through life, many of us slip into procrastination very easily. If you find that you procrastinate, you are not alone. SOS self-help methods can help in reducing this tendency. The *ABC View Of Our Emotions* helps explain our tendency to procrastinate.

ABC View Of Our Emotions & Behavior

A ——— Activates/Triggers ——— B ——— Causes ———> C

Activating Event   Beliefs & Self-Talk   Consequences:
                                                   Emotional & Behavioral
Avoided actions   Procrastination
or chores

The avoided action or anticipated situation about which we are procrastinating, such as cleaning out the garage, is the A activating event. Our procrastination, frustration, and discouragement are C consequences: emotional and behavioral.

Our B beliefs and self-talk cause our procrastination. Which irrational beliefs and self-talk are most likely to cause us to procrastinate?

Irrational belief #7 (from Chapter Six), stated below, particularly accounts for our tendency to procrastinate. The following also describes the typical consequences of holding that belief and discusses helpful alternative beliefs.

7. It's easier to avoid and to put off facing life's difficulties and responsibilities than to face them.

It's awful and I-can't-stand the frustration of dealing with situations and hassles that I should not have to deal with. Difficulties and hassles should be condemned & damned.

Typical Consequences - Procrastination & guilt; small problems turn into large problems; one feels overwhelmed with multiplying difficulties; frustration tolerance is lowered; one's major goals become jeopardized; self-defeating behavior results; often anxiety and depression result.

Rational Alternative Beliefs - *Dealing with responsibilities, hassles, and chores is a part of life. Attending to problems in their early stages is inconvenient, but hardly awful. I-can-stand dealing with problems as they occur. Dealing with responsibilities now actually makes life easier. I can begin a task even though I "don't feel like it."*

Irrational Beliefs And Self-talk (B's) Causing Procrastination

- *"Doing these disagreeable actions will cause me too much frustration."*

- *"My emotional discomfort will be too much to bear."*

- *"The world must be easy. I should not have to deal with problems and chores because they are too hard."*

- *"Dealing with a problem is HTA (horrible, terrible, awful)."*

- *"It's easier to avoid and to put off facing life's difficulties and responsibilities than to face them."*

- *"I-can't-stand to risk trying and then failing because I would lose my self-respect and respect from others."*

- *I should wait until I "feel like doing it."*

Avoid Perfectionism

Perfectionism is a tendency or disposition to regard anything short of perfection as unacceptable. Perfectionism demands unrealistically high standards in ourselves and in our work (Dryden & Neenan, 1994). To strive for excellence in a variety of tasks isn't unhealthy. *However, it's unhealthy to judge myself as worthy or acceptable only if I reach perfection in most tasks.*

Perfectionism can cause procrastination since perfection is an unattainable goal. A perfectionistic individual usually has much difficulty in starting a task or in finishing it.

Irrational belief #2 (from Chapter Six) often leads to perfectionism. The following describes the usual consequences of holding that irrational belief. Rational alternative beliefs are also given.

> **# 2. I must be thoroughly competent, adequate, and achieving in all important respects, in order to be worthwhile.**
> I must be 100% competent in all important areas and if I am not as I must be, its awful, I-can't-stand-it, I'm worthless, and I should be condemned. It would be horrible to be merely average.

Typical Consequences - Anxiety, depression, low self-acceptance, low self-esteem, procrastination.

Rational Alternative Beliefs - *I'm an imperfect, fallible person who has both strengths and limitations. I will work toward improving myself. There are things I do well. I can learn from my mistakes and from the hard knocks of life.*

PERFECTIONISM CAN CAUSE PROCRASTINATION

Helping Ourselves
Requires Study And Practice

Study and repeatedly practice the many self-help methods presented in *SOS Help For Emotions*. Especially, do the following:

- Copy and complete the ABCDE Self-Analysis And Improvement Form when you find yourself becoming distressed about unpleasant events or people. Do this even when you have difficulty identifying your unpleasant activating events. The use of this form is illustrated in Chapters Five, Seven, Eight, Nine, and Ten.

    You'll also need to review frequently the ABC View Of Our Emotions to understand and improve your emotions when you feel upset.

- Complete the Daily Mood Record when you feel distressed. This record of your mood will prompt you to identify activating events and beliefs causing you distress. The Daily Mood Record is described in Chapters Three, Seven, Eight, and Nine.

- Study and practice the suggestions presented in the various chapters. A mere casual reading of SOS is insufficient to bring about the personal changes in which you are interested.

- Complete the quizzes and exercises in Chapter 12. This will help you to evaluate your understanding of the *SOS* methods of self-help.

- Consider reading one of the self-help books listed in this chapter.

- Consider getting professional help.

- Obtain information from one of the mental health organizations listed in this chapter.

- Beware of excuses and irrational beliefs blocking you from applying and repeatedly practicing the self-help methods you have learned. One excuse is not allowing enough time to practice the exercises. Other irrational beliefs which may prevent you from studying and applying what you have learned from *SOS Help For Emotions* are the following:

  #5. **There isn't much I can do about my anxiety, anger, depression, or unhappiness, because my feelings are caused by what happens to me.**

  #9. **My past history mainly causes my present feelings and behavior; things from my past which once strongly influenced me will always strongly influence me.**

- Avoid procrastination and perfectionism.

- Deal with the world as it is, not as it "must be" or "should be."

- Forcefully and repeatedly dispute those irrational beliefs which discourage you from managing and improving your emotions.
  Accept the fact that there will be periods of time when you will have reduced ability to manage your emotions. Don't condemn yourself when stressful events pile up, and you begin backsliding and want to give up. As soon as you're able, recover and return to managing your emotions more effectively.

- When bad events occur, change what you can and accept what you can't change.

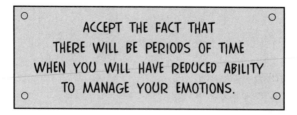

ACCEPT THE FACT THAT
THERE WILL BE PERIODS OF TIME
WHEN YOU WILL HAVE REDUCED ABILITY
TO MANAGE YOUR EMOTIONS.

PSYCHOLOGY   SELF-HELP BOOKS   SELF-IMPROVEMENT

JR

"Oh, I don't need a book for improving <u>myself</u>! What have you got for improving <u>others</u>? I've got a list here of people who need to change."

Self-Help Resources

SOS Help For Emotions: Managing Anxiety, Anger, And Depression is based on the psychotherapy method called *rational emotive behavior therapy (REBT), cognitive behavior therapy, and ABC View Of Emotions.* Additional self-help books are listed below.

The Merck Manual Of Medical Information: Second Home Edition (2003) at <www.merck.com/pubs/mmanual> is my favorite book and website for information on health problems and treatments. The website is a valuable free resource, although somewhat technical. For information on a variety of medications go to <www.drugdigest.org>.

Rational Emotive Behavior Therapy - REBT Books
(REBT therapy forms the foundation for *SOS Help For Emotions*.)

Borcherdt, B. (1989). *Think Straight! Feel Great! 21 Guides To Emotional Self-Control.* Sarasota, FL: Professional   Resource Exchange.

Ellis, A. (1991). *Dealing With Difficult People.* Audiocassette recording. New York: Institute for Rational-Emotive Therapy. The speaker is Ellis.

Ellis, A. (1992). *How To Stubbornly Refuse To Make Yourself Miserable About Anything — Yes Anything!* Secaucus, NJ: Lyle Stuart.

Nottingham, E. (2001). *It's Not As Bad As It Seems.* Writer's Club Press.

Wolfe, J. (1992). *What To Do When He Has A Headache.* New York: Hyperion. Available from Albert Ellis Institute For Rational Emotive Therapy. Especially written for women, this book helps improve relationships and communication between men and women.

Various REBT self-help books and tapes are available from Albert Ellis Institute For Rational Emotive Behavior Therapy, 45 East 65th Street, New York, NY 10021. Telephone is (212)535-0822 or (800)323-4738. Ask for a catalog. The website is <http://www.rebt.org>

Other Cognitive Behavior Therapy Books
Burns, D. (1999). *Feeling Good: The New Mood Therapy.* New York: Avon Books. David Burns' website is<http://www.feelinggood.com>

Guide To Self-Help Books, Support Groups, And Internet
Norcross, J., Santrock, J., Campbell, L., Smith, T., Sommer, R., & Zukerman, E. (2000). *The Authoritative Guide to Self-Help Resources in Mental Health.* New York: Guilford Press. This is an excellent guide to hundreds of self-help books, internet sites, and support groups. Books are recommended for addictions, divorce, eating disorders, and 20 additional categories. Available at many libraries, it is intended for mental health professionals and the general public.

Assertiveness
Alberti, R. & Emmons, M. (2001). *Your Perfect Right, 8th Ed.* San Luis Obispo, CA: Impact Publishers. This book helps individuals to stand up for their rights and manage interpersonal problems with appropriate assertiveness.

Coping With Difficult People
Bramson, R. (1981). *Coping With Difficult People.* New York: Ballatine Books. The focus is on dealing with difficult supervisors, co-workers, and customers in the workplace.

An audiotape based on this book and by the same name is available from Simon & Schuster Publishing Division.

Relationships

Bolton, R. (1979). *People Skills.* New York: Touchstone. Various communication skills are taught including listening skills, assertiveness, and conflict-resolution skills.

Carnegie, D. (1998). *How To Win Friends And Influence People, Rev. ed.* New York: Pocket Books. Mental health professionals give this book mixed reviews, but in my opinion, it is particularly helpful for initiating and improving relationships. Over 15 million copies have been sold since it was originally published.

Tannen, D. (1990). *You Just Don't Understand: Women And Men In Conversation.* New York: Ballantine. The book focuses on how women and men differ in their style of communication and how communication can be improved.

Self-Motivation And Achieving Goals

Covey, S. (1989). *The 7 Habits Of Effective People.* New York: Simon & Schuster. Covey presents seven basic habits, important in achieving one's goals.

Bolles, R. (2001). *What Color Is Your Parachute?* Berkeley, CA: Ten Speed Press. This book is especially valuable for people changing careers, seeking a job, or developing a career.

Parenting Young Children

Clark, L. (1996 with 2003 Revisions). *SOS help for parents: A practical guide for handling common everyday behavior problems, 2nd Ed.* Bowling Green, KY: SOS Programs & Parents Press. Illustrated and available in English, Spanish (2002), Korean, Chinese (from Taiwan), Chinese (from Beijing Normal University), Hungarian, Turkish, Icelandic, and Arabic. Over 20 practical methods and skills are presented for

helping parents and teachers to manage behavior
problems of children between two and twelve.
   The Video SOS Help For Parents, also available in
Spanish, is used by counselors and educators for parent
counseling and parent education workshops. For more
information, see the end pages of this book and
<http://www.sosprograms.com>

Faber, A. & Mazlish, E. (1999). *How To Talk So Kids Will
   Listen & Listen So Kids Will Talk.* New York: Avon.
   This book helps parents to communicate more
   effectively with their children.

Schaefer, C. (1994). *How To Talk To Your Kids About Really
   Important Things: For Children Four to Twelve.* San
   Francisco, CA: Jossey-Bass Publishers.
   This unique book gives parents the words to use when
   talking to children about more than thirty important,
   sensitive questions. Some questions included are: a
   new baby in the home, going to the doctor, repeating a
   grade, and pornography. It is an essential book for
   parents of young children, in my opinion.

Parenting Adolescents
Dinkmeyer, D. & McKay, G. (1990). *Parenting Teenagers:
   Systematic Training For Effective Parenting Of Teens.*
   Circle Pines, MN: American Guidance Service.

Schaefer, C. (1999). *How to talk to teens about really important
   things: Specific questions and answers and useful things
   to say.* San Francisco, CA: Jossey-Bass Publishers.
   This is an essential book for parents of teenagers. Some
   of the questions include drinking and driving, AIDS, tatoos,
   cults, gangs, depression, ect.

When And How To Get Professional Help

   Mental health professionals can help us to accept
what we can't change, to help change what we can, and to
help us know the difference.

The journey from childhood to old age is long and often difficult. Bad events occur and our evaluation of those events can lead to long-term anxiety, anger, depression, and other unhealthy and destructive feelings. Our irrational beliefs and unhealthy feelings can block us from achieving contentment and attaining our goals.

If difficulties persist in spite of your best efforts to resolve them, avoid giving in to anxiety, hopelessness, inactivity, guilt, depression, or anger. Contact a therapist or counselor for professional help. Consider the following questions when thinking about counseling.

Q: *"When should I get professional help?"*

A: Consider getting professional help if you are persistently unhappy or having significant difficulty in social or family relationships. You may also benefit from professional help if you are experiencing significant difficulty in adjusting to work or school demands.

Q: *"How do I learn about professional counseling services in my area?"*

A: It takes effort to learn about competent counselors and appropriate helping agencies in your community. Ask your physician to recommend the names of at least two counselors. Also discuss the possible benefit of a physical examination since various medical conditions can cause emotional difficulties.

Other sources of information about therapists or agencies include the clergy or friends. Most telephone crisis or help lines and community mental health centers are valuable sources of information. Telephone directories list psychiatrists, psychologists, psychotherapists, marriage and family counselors, and clinical social workers.

Professionals who offer therapy and counseling include: psychiatrists (M.D.), psychologists (Ph.D., Psy.D., M.A., or M.S.), clinical social workers

(M.S.W., L.C.S.W.), and licensed counselors. Most states require that mental health professionals be certified or licensed.

Q: *"What do I ask the counselor during our first contact?"*

A: After obtaining the names of a couple of counselors or counseling services, you'll need to telephone a counselor or an agency. If the counselor is in independent practice ask to speak directly with the counselor. Briefly, tell the counselor the nature of your difficulties. Mention that you understand that cognitive therapy can be particularly helpful. Also say you have been reading *SOS Help For Emotions* which has a cognitive therapy orientation.

Ask if the counselor can help individuals with the difficulties you have described. If not, ask whom she would recommend. Inquire about her training, experience, and certification for offering counseling or therapy.

Ask about the cost of each visit, the length of counseling sessions, how many visits will probably be necessary, and over what period of time. At least six to ten sessions are usually necessary.

When first beginning counseling or therapy, it's important to schedule weekly visits of at least 45 minutes duration. It's not helpful to begin counseling with once a month sessions or with sessions lasting only 20 or 30 minutes. Most psychiatrists do not have the time to see clients in regular counseling or therapy sessions. For counseling they usually refer their clients to counselors and therapists.

Q: *"Is medication for anxiety or depression helpful?"*

A: Antianxiety or antidepressant medication often can help anxiety, depression, anxiety disorders, and depressive disorders. However, it's important to start counseling along with medication.

The choice of whether or not you take medication is with you and a physician. Only a psychiatrist or other physician can prescribe medication. Most therapists have a working relationship with a physician who will evaluate clients for medication.

Q: *"How do I pay for professional services?"*

A: Counseling and therapy cost money, but so do health care, education, transportation, entertainment, eating out, and vacations. Many health plans pay for therapy or for a given number of sessions. Check with your insurance company or have your therapist check. Also, consider paying for sessions yourself.

Q: *"Do most therapists use REBT therapy or another cognitive behavior therapy approach in helping clients?"*

A: Considerable evidence supports the value of cognitive behavior therapy approaches. Therapists of various orientations include methods from REBT and cognitive behavior therapy in their practice. A number of effective treatments are used to help clients. The effectiveness of therapy largely depends on the training and experience of the therapist, as well as, on the effort of the client.

"No progress in therapy!"

Jennifer told me how she felt like "such a failure" because she had made "no progress in therapy" even though she had been meeting with a psychiatrist and receiving medication for nearly two years.

I asked, *"How often do you see him?"* She replied, *"once a month."* *"How long are your appointments,"* I inquired. Jennifer said, *"About 10 minutes. He asks me how I'm doing, writes some notes, hands me another prescription for medication, and then I leave."*

I was disappointed at what I heard! Jennifer actually is getting "medication only," but believes she also is getting therapy. I explained that individual therapy sessions are usually 50 minutes with group sessions being longer. I suggested that she talk with her psychiatrist about finding a way to receive talking therapy, as well as medication.

Psychiatrists who regularly meet with patients, but only offer medication due to time constraints, are usually willing to arrange for their patients to also meet with a counselor for talking therapy.

Four Ways To Receive Help

• Individual therapy – *A therapist meets with one client in individual therapy.* In cognitive behavior therapies, clients are asked to study cognitive therapy self-help materials such as *SOS Help For Emotions.**

• Group therapy – *A therapist meets with several individuals in group therapy.* Group therapy is often recommended after individual therapy sessions have been completed. It's more cost efficient than individual therapy and has other advantages as well. Individuals gain experience helping each other to recognize and apply principles such as the *three major musts, the five hot links, disputing irrational beliefs, changing demands into preferences*, etc. The group can help individuals identify feelings which are at a low level of awareness. Cognitive therapists usually ask group members to study cognitive self-help materials.

• Marriage counseling – *The counselor meets with both partners in marriage counseling or relationship counseling.* Improving the irrational beliefs and low frustration tolerance in both partners can help improve a relationship.

• Family therapy – *A therapist meets jointly with all members of a family in family therapy.* Many family

---

* In REBT therapy, it is important that the client learn REBT concepts such as the ABC View Of Emotions. Many cognitive behavior therapy concepts and methods are taught in *SOS Help For Emotions.*

therapists believe the best way to resolve both individual problems and relationship problems is by meeting with all family members at one time.

Questions About REBT Therapy, Moral Values, Prayer, And Religion

Q: "When working with clients, some REBT therapists use considerable profanity. Why?"

A: Albert Ellis, the founder of REBT therapy is well known to therapists for his use of earthy language and profanity (Dryden & Neeman, 1994).*Ellis believes that the use of profanity by the therapist helps build a therapeutic relationship and serves to emphasize important points. Some REBT therapists believe profanity facilitates the client's recognition and expression of unpleasant feelings. However, many therapists and clients feel that a considerable amount of swearing by the therapist is offensive and not helpful to therapy. Many therapists believe swearing a lot is practicing getting upset and angry.

Q: "What is the view of REBT therapy regarding guilt?"**

A: Breaking your moral code is a major cause of guilt. REBT believes that remorse and regret need to be substituted for guilt. Also, the individual can resolve to improve his behavior in the future.
      Guilt is the belief: *"I must not have done that (a bad act). Since I did; it's awful; I-can't-stand-it; and I'm a rotten person."*
      The rational alternatives to guilt are remorse or regret. Remorse and regret involve the rational

---

• For brief discussions of morals, religion, profanity, and REBT therapy see *Dictionary Of Rational Emotive Behaviour Therapy* by Dryden & Neeman (1994). Also see, "Pros and cons of using profanity," in The RET Resource Book For Practitioners (Bernard & Wolfe, 1993).

•• Don Beal contributed ideas to the issue of REBT therapy and guilt.

belief: *"I prefer that I had not done that act. That act is very bad. I'm very sorry that I did it, truly sorry. And while I don't like it one bit, I-can-stand-it, but I don't like it that I did that act. While my behavior was very bad, I am not a thoroughly bad person. Rather, I am a complex, fallible human being who behaved badly. I had better make amends, and then I had better figure out what led me to this behavior so that I won't do it again in the future."*

The Christian faith provides additional ways to resolve guilt. These include confession and forgiveness. I don't see any basic conflict between REBT and Christianity.

Q: "What does REBT therapy say about prayer?"

A: When people of various faiths pray they usually ask for the bad events (As) to end or for their miserable feelings (Cs) to lessen. However, people also need to ask for help and encouragement in attaining more rational, self-helping beliefs and self-talk (Bs) which mainly cause their feelings (Cs). This point is made in an excellent book by Nielsen, Johnson, and Ellis (2001).

> GOD GRANT ME
> SERENITY TO ACCEPT THE THINGS I CANNOT CHANGE,
> COURAGE TO CHANGE THE THINGS I CAN,
> AND
> WISDOM TO KNOW THE DIFFERENCE.

Mental Health Organizations

Consider contacting the following organizations for information about adjustment problems, emotional disorders, counseling, therapy, or self-help methods (Hales & Hales, 1995). Most of these organizations will provide printed material about emotional problems, disorders, or treatments. In some cases they provide names of therapists and self-help groups.

Anxiety Disorders Association of America
11900 Parklawn Drive, Suite 100, Rockville, MD 20852. Telephone (301)231-9350. For anxiety disorders. <http://www.adaa.org>

National Alliance for the Mentally Ill
Colonial Place Three, 2107 Wilson Blvd, Suite 300, Arlington, VA 22201. Telephone (800) 950-6264. <http://www.nami.org> Self-help and advocacy organization for persons with a variety of mental disorders and for their families.

National Depressive and Manic-Depressive Association
730 North Franklin Street, Suite 501, Chicago, IL, 60610. Telephone (800) 826-3632. Manic-Depressive Disorder is also called Bipolar Disorder. <http://www.ndmda.org>
National Family Caregivers Association
10400 Connecticut Ave, Suite 500, Kensington, MD 20895. Telephone (301) 942-6430. This organization is especially for families of individuals with disorders. <http://www.nfcacares.org>

As previously mentioned, the basis of *SOS Help For Emotions: Managing Anxiety, Anger, And Depression* is rational emotive behavior therapy*. More information about REBT is available from the following organization.
Albert Ellis Institute For Rational Emotive Behavior Therapy, 45 East 65th Street, New York, NY 10021. Telephone is (212)535-0822 or (800)323-4738. Ask for a catalog. The web site is <http://www.rebt.org>

Main Points To Remember:

• Avoid procrastination and perfectionism.

---

*Rational emotive behavior therapy and *SOS Help For Emotions* are both a part of cognitive behavior therapy.

- Deal with the world as it is, not as it "must be" or "should be."

- When bad events occur, accept what you can't change, change what you can, and strive to know the difference.

- Recognize that mental health professionals can help us to change what we can change and to accept what we can't change.

- Complete the quizzes and exercises in Chapter 12.

- Beware of excuses and irrational beliefs blocking you from applying and practicing the many self-help methods you have learned from SOS.

- Do read and study self-help materials in your area of concern. *The Authoritative Guide to Self-Help Resources in Mental Health* can help you to evaluate self-help resources.

- *Accept the fact that there will be periods of time when you will have reduced ability to manage your emotions.* Don't condemn yourself when stressful events pile up, and you begin backsliding and wanting to give up. As soon as you're able, recover and return to managing your emotions more effectively.

- Test your understanding of Chapters 10 and 11 and of prior chapters. Turn to Chapter 12 and complete Part Four of the quizzes and exercises.

The Merck Manual Of Medical Information: Second Home Edition at <www.merck.com/pubs/mmanual> is my favorite book and website for information on health problems and treatments. The website is a valuable free resource, although somewhat technical. For information on a variety of medications go to <www.drugdigest.org>.

Chapter 12

Quizzes And Exercises

To evaluate your understanding of SOS, complete the quizzes and exercises in this chapter. To achieve actual positive change in your thoughts, feelings, and behavior, you'll need to repeatedly practice the exercises and methods taught in SOS. Increasing your skill in tennis takes practice. Likewise, increasing your ability to know and manage your emotions, requires practice of what you have learned.

After responding to the questions in Part One, compare your answers with the answers provided. For additional feedback or help regarding the exercises, refer to Chapters One, Two, and Three.

If you have borrowed this book or plan to lend it to others, consider marking your answers on photocopies of these pages.

PART ONE QUIZZES AND EXERCISES
COVERING CHAPTERS 1, 2, & 3.

Part One <u>Questions</u> covering Chapters One, Two, and Three. Select the one best answer to the following questions. Some questions are easy and some are difficult. No one is expected to get them all correct.

1.   Our "fight or flight" response:
      a. made life easier for saber-toothed tigers.
      b. was not helpful to our ancestors.
      c. can cause problems in adapting to the modern world.
      d. wasn't possible until people could fly in the
         twentieth century.

2.   Our four core emotions are:
      a. depression, contentment, anxiety, and frustration.
      b. contentment, depression, anxiety, and anger.
      c. depression, anxiety, anger, and more anger.
      d. anxiety, fear, anger, and low self-esteem.

3.   Our emotions are largely, but not entirely, controlled by:
      a. unpleasant situations.
      b. unpleasant situations and difficult people.
      c. our genetic makeup and childhood experiences.
      d. our beliefs and self-talk.

4.   Our job success and positive evaluations by supervisors is
      highly related to our:
      a. good luck.
      b. emotional intelligence.
      c. the position of the stars at our birth.
      d. general intelligence.

5.   The letters REBT stand for:
      a. reality effort behavior therapy.
      b. rational emotive behavior therapy.
      c. responsibility emotions behavior thinking.
      d. reality empathy balance theory.

6.   Which of the following is <u>false</u>?
      a. beliefs and self-talk are what we believe and tell
            ourselves about activating events.
      b. beliefs and self-talk are both rational and irrational.
      c. beliefs and self-talk include only rational beliefs.
      d. beliefs and self-talk are activated or awakened by
            activating events.

7.   Our C consequences of emotions and behaviors are caused
      by:
      a. events and situations.
      b. beliefs and self-talk about events and situations.
      c. genetics, heredity, and early childhood experiences.
      d. how others treat us.

8.   Believing that A activating events directly cause C
      consequences of emotions and behaviors is called:
      a. straight thinking.
      b. A–B–C thinking.
      c. healthy thinking.
      d. crooked thinking

9.   To live contentedly requires:
      a. knowing the ABC's of our emotions.
      b. considerable luck.
      c. ignorance and a naive attitude.
      d. a high IQ or a good education.

10. Which of the following major musts leads to emotional distress?
    a. You (he or she) must!
    b. The world and the conditions under which I live must!
    c. I must!
    d. all of the above lead to emotional distress.

11. Which of the following choices is <u>not</u> one of the five hot connecting links?
    a. awfulizing.
    b. I-can't-stand-it-itis.
    c. preferences and wishes.
    d. I'm worthless.

12. What connects the three major musts to unhealthy, unpleasant emotions?
    a. always & never.
    b. condemnation & damnation.
    c. I'm worthless.
    d. all of the above can connect the three major musts to unhealthy, unpleasant emotions.
    e. none of the above can connect the three major musts to unhealthy, unpleasant emotions.

13. What is a primary cause of emotional distress?
    a. advancing our wishes and desires to absolute shoulds and demands.
    b. keeping our wishes and desires as wishes and desires.
    c. acknowledging to ourselves that we have wishes and desires.
    d. acknowledging to others that we have wishes and desires.

14. Our irrational beliefs originate from:
    a. our parents and family.
    b. society-at-large.
    c. mass media.
    d. our own peculiar thinking.
    e. all of the above.

15. Which of the following self-talk statements reflects rational A–B–C thinking, taking responsibility for our own negative feelings?
    a. "She hurt my feelings by what she said."
    b. "My boss really made me mad and the more I thought about what he did, the madder I got."
    c. "I got myself all upset over that clerk's behavior
    d. "It made me depressed all day after he told me about that terrible experience he had."

Answers to Part One Questions:
1c 2b 3d 4b 5b 6c 7b 8d 9a 10d 11c 12d 13a 14e 15c

Part One Exercises covering Chapters 1, 2, & 3. Copy and complete.

Exercise A:
   What do the following letters stand for?
         A _____
         B _____
         C _____

Exercise B:
   The three basic musts are:

         _____
         _____
         _____

Exercise C:
   List as many of the five hot connecting links as possible. (Remember CIA, IA.)

         _____
         _____
         _____
         _____
         _____

Exercise D:
   The four basic emotions are:

         _____
         _____
         _____
         _____

Exercise E:
   Copy the "A—B—C Self-Analysis Form." Select a recent situation with which you are (or were) upset and then complete this form.

A—B—C Self-Analysis Form

Date: _____

A <u>Activating</u> <u>Event</u> (Unpleasant event or situation; can be anticipated events):

B <u>Beliefs</u> **And Self-Talk Statements** (Your irrational beliefs and self-talk statements; especially your musts, absolute shoulds, and five hot links):

C <u>Consequences:</u> **Emotional & Behavioral** (Your unpleasant emotion and maladaptive behavior): Emotions:

Behavior (or contemplated behavior):

The following are steps for doing an ABC Self-Analysis.

First, enter what you think is your A activating event.

Second, write in your C consequences: emotions and behaviors.

Third, listen closely to your B beliefs and self-talk-statements. Then write in your suspected irrational beliefs and self-talk statements. Especially look for your use of the three major musts and shoulds and your use of the five hot connecting links (I-can't-stand-it-itis, etc.). *Detecting your B Beliefs and Self-Talk Statements is the most challenging part of your analysis.*

Exercise F:

Copy this "Daily Mood Record." For today, enter your estimated average mood for anxiety, anger, and depression. Also write a few notes regarding your mood for today.

Daily Mood Record:
Record Of Anxiety, Anger, And Depression

On a scale from 1 to 10 write in a number corresponding to your estimated average mood for the day. Mild is 1 to 3, moderate is 4 to 5, high is 6 to 8, and severe is 9 to 10.

Date/ Time	Anxiety	Anger	Depres- sion	Notes

The following directions describe how to keep a Daily Mood Record.

First, decide which of the basic emotions you are going to log. Pay close attention to those emotions. Record your approximate average mood for the emotions you have decided to track. Do this each day. Enter any notes on the record that might help you to better understand your emotions.

READ, STUDY, PRACTICE

PART TWO QUIZZES AND EXERCISES
COVERING CHAPTERS 4, 5, & 6

Part Two Questions covering Chapters Four, Five, and Six. Photocopy and complete. Select the one best answer to the following questions. Some questions are easy and some are difficult. No one is expected to get them all correct.

1. The three major musts:
   a. include preferences and wishes.
   b. lead to emotional stability.
   c. include shoulds and oughts.
   d. help us to achieve our goals.

2. Managing our emotions is a big part of:
   a. our emotional intelligence.
   b. success in achieving our goals.
   c. our happiness.
   d. all of the above are correct.

3. An example of an emotional problem (rather than a practical problem) is:
   a. poor grades.
   b. running two months behind on the rent.
   c. not having a date for Saturday night.
   d. anxiety about having only 50 dollars in the checking account.
   e. all of the above are correct.

4. Regarding practical problems and emotional problems,
   a. it's best to deal with the emotional problem before the practical problem.
   b. it's best to deal with the practical problem before the emotional problem.
   c. it doesn't make any difference which one is dealt with first.
   d. nearly all problems are impossible to deal with.

5. Which of the following is a true statement?
   a. it's best to set a goal of how you want to feel and act in response to difficult situations.
   b. it's best to choose a "role model" from violent action movies.
   c. whom you choose as a "role model" doesn't have any influence on your behavior or emotions.
   d. none of the above is a true statement.

6.   Helping yourself to feel annoyance instead of anger or
      rage is called:
      a. deciding on a goal for your emotions.
      b. practicing mental imagery.
      c. self-deceptive and absurd.
      d. replacing unhealthy emotions with healthy ones.

7.   Changing your demands and musts into wishes and
      preferences:
      a. is unhealthy.
      b. increases frustration.
      c. is ridiculous.
      d. is healthy.

8.   The statement, "I don't like it, that's ok, I can stand it any
      way," is called:
      a. distraction and diversion.
      b. coping self-talk statement.
      c. mental imagery.
      d. an activating event.

9.   Knowing our irrational beliefs and self-talk is:
      a. essential to managing our emotions.
      b. important in avoiding emotional problems.
      c. helpful in soothing our emotions.
      d. all of the above are correct.

10.   Rational beliefs, as opposed to irrational beliefs:
      a. include the five hot links.
      b. are self-helping, logical, reality-based, and useful.
      c. are normally based on shoulds, musts, and oughts.
      d. are not much fun.

11.   Asking yourself, "What am I saying to myself about myself
      or about others?" is an example of:
      a. disputing and debating irrational beliefs.
      b. detecting and identifying irrational beliefs.
      c. an activating event.
      d. consequences, emotional and behavioral.

12. How long do you need to debate an irrational belief?
    a. until you get annoyed with yourself.
    b. until you detect another irrational belief.
    c. until the irrational belief argues back.
    d. until you no longer believe it.

13. Believing the world is too hard <u>and</u> telling yourself, "I can't stand it being so hard," is:
    a. frustration.
    b. low frustration tolerance.
    c. rational thinking.
    d. calming and soothing yourself.
    e. low self-acceptance.

14. Saying to yourself, "I don't think I will lose my job, but if I do I can stand it. And I will get another one," is an example of:
    a. positive thinking.
    b. frustration.
    c. rational thinking.
    d. unrealistic, irrational thinking.

15. Believing, "The world absolutely must be fair to me," is an example of:
    a. setting yourself up to feel miserable.
    b. irrational thinking.
    c. a cause of anger, anxiety, and depression.
    d. all of the above are true.

Answers to Part Two Questions:
1c   2d   3d   4a   5a   6d   7d   8b   9d   10b   11b   12d   13b   14c   15d

(Part Two Exercises — see the next page)

Part Two Exercises covering Chapters 4, 5, & 6. Copy and complete.

Exercise A:
   Write in the missing names on the eight lines.

ABC View Of Our Emotions

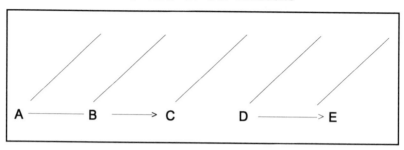

Exercise B:

   How Self-Talk Causes Emotions. Fill in the lines.
   Three Major Musts are:
   1 _____
   2 _____
   3 _____

        Five Hot Links (remember CIA, IA) are:
        1 _____
        2 _____
        3 _____
        4 _____
        5 _____

             Three Main Unhealthy Emotions are:
             1 _____
             2 _____
             3 _____

Exercise C:
   Copy the "ABCDE Self-Analysis And Improvement Form."
   Select a recent situation with which you were (or are)
   upset and complete the entire form.

ABCDE
Self-Analysis And Improvement Form

Date:

A Activating Event (Unpleasant event or situation; can be anticipated events):

B Beliefs And Self-Talk Statements (Your irrational beliefs and self-talk statements; especially your musts, absolute shoulds, and five hot links):

C Consequences: Emotional & Behavioral (Your unpleasant emotion and maladaptive behavior):
Emotions:

Behavior (or contemplated behavior):

D Dispute And Debate (Dispute your irrational beliefs and self-talk; especially your musts, absolute shoulds, and five hot links):

E Effects (Effects Of Dispute: New emotions and behaviors):

Copy this form. Complete the steps in the order of A, C, B, D, and E. When upset, follow the self-help methods in Chapters 4, 5, and other chapters. As you complete B, look for your musts, absolute shoulds, hot links, and the 11 irrational beliefs described in Chapter Six.

PART THREE QUIZZES AND EXERCISES
COVERING CHAPTERS 7, 8, & 9

Part Three Questions covering Chapters Seven, Eight, and Nine. Photocopy and complete. Select the one best answer to the following questions. Some questions are easy and some are difficult. No one is expected to get them all correct.

1.   Basic feelings and emotions which cause people considerable distress are:
      a. anger.
      b. depression.
      c. anxiety and fear.
      d. all of the above.

2.   What can contribute to an anxiety disorder?
      a. medical problems and conditions.
      b. bad situations.
      c. irrational beliefs.
      d. all of the above.

3.   When feeling worried, tense, or anxious, it's important to:
      a. distract ourselves by thinking about something else.
      b. acknowledge that our beliefs and self-talk mainly cause our emotions.
      c. acknowledge that most bad events are the cause of our emotional problems.
      d. find the person who is responsible for making us feel this way and deal directly with that person.

4.   *SOS Help For Emotions* is based on:
      a. ABC view of our emotions.
      b. rational emotive behavior therapy.
      c. both of the above.
      d. none of the above.

5.   When coping with anxiety it's especially important to:
      a. deal first with the emotional problem.
      b. replace major musts with preferences and wishes.
      c. use coping self-talk statements.
      d. drop any of the five hot links that you are using.
      e. all of the above are especially important.

6. When feeling upset and anxious, one of the worst things you could do is to:
    a. consider a trial period on antianxiety medication.
    b. consider having a physical exam.
    c. use alcohol or "recreational" drugs.
    d. meet with a therapist.

7. Of the following emotions, which is least frequently admitted as being an emotional problem?
    a. anxiety.
    b. anger.
    c. depression.
    d. poor mechanical aptitude.

8. Experiencing "considerable emotional distress or significant impairment in relationships with others or significant impairment as a wage earner, homemaker, or student," is a description of:
    a. a long-suffering individualist.
    b. an emotional problem.
    c. an emotional disorder.
    d. none of the above is correct.

9. Anger is primarily determined by:
    a. other people acting badly, wrongfully, and inconsiderately.
    b. an unfair world.
    c. an adrenalin surge or rush.
    d. what we believe and tell ourselves about bad events.

10. An unpleasant situation which you believe has made you angry is called:
    a. consequences of emotions and behavior.
    b. an activating event.
    c. beliefs and self-talk.
    d. dispute and debate.

11. What is the best method for managing your anger so that it is less upsetting to you?
    a. saying to yourself, "I don't get angry."
    b. holding the anger in and letting it dissipate.
    c. letting the anger out and expressing it.
    d. turning the anger down.

12. A prime "trigger" for one's anger is:
    a. low frustration tolerance.
    b. a threat to our self-worth.
    c. valuing toughness and aggression.
    d. all of the above are prime triggers.

13. A prime "trigger" for one's depression is:
    a. thinking about the possibility of losing something important in the future.
    b. the loss of something important.
    c. accepting the loss of something important, without demanding that it must not have happened.
    d. none of the above is a prime trigger for depression.

14. The primary way to deal with low self-esteem is to:
    a. set up a program to improve your personal characteristics and accomplishments.
    b. work on getting more people to like you.
    c. work on gaining self-acceptance.
    d. go to a summer camp that builds self-esteem.

15. Most serious emotional problems stem from:
    a. irrational beliefs and thoughts.
    b. emotional trauma and a psychologically impoverished childhood.
    c. poor communication skills and impaired social skills.
    d. unconscious sexual and aggressive needs and motives.

Answers to Part Three Questions:
1d 2d 3b 4c 5e 6c 7b 8c 9d 10b 11d 12d 13b 14c 15a

```
read, study, practice
```

(Part Three Exercises – see next page.)

Part Three Exercises covering Chapters 7, 8, 9, and prior chapters. Some exercises have been given previously. Copy and complete.

Exercise A:
>   Write in the missing names on the eight lines.

ABC View Of Our Emotions

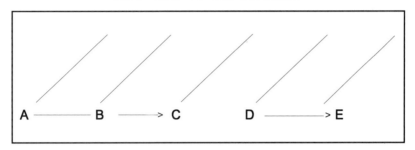

Exercise B:
>   How Self-Talk Causes Emotions. Fill in the lines.
>   Three Major Musts are:
>   1 _____
>   2 _____
>   3 _____
>
>   Five Hot Links (remember CIA, IA) are:
>   1 _____
>   2 _____
>   3 _____
>   4 _____
>   5 _____
>
>   Three Main Unhealthy Emotions are:
>   1 _____
>   2 _____
>   3 _____

Exercise C:
>   Copy the "ABCDE Self-Analysis And Improvement Form."
>   Select a recent situation with which you were (or are)
>   upset and complete the entire form.

PART FOUR QUIZZES AND EXERCISES
COVERING CHAPTERS 10 & 11

Part Four Questions covering Chapters 10 & 11. Photocopy and complete. Select the one best answer to the following questions. Some questions are easy and some are difficult. No one is expected to get them all correct.

1.   If you become emotionally upset while dealing with a difficult person, it's important to:
   a. deal first with your distress and then with the difficult person.
   b. deal first with the difficult person and then with your distress.
   c. not give in to the demands of a difficult person as it will only reinforce that person's difficult behavior.
   d. avoid difficult people.

2.   In the ABC view of our emotions, the behavior of a difficult person can be considered as:
   a. consequences of emotions and behavior.
   b. an activating event.
   c. beliefs and self-talk.
   d. dispute and debate.
   e. HTA (horrible, terrible, awful).

3.   It's not unpleasant people who cause our distress but rather:
   a. their behavior and what they say.
   b. their actual motives and intentions.
   c. our beliefs and self-talk about their behavior and intentions.
   d. the impact that their behavior has on our lives.

4.   In the ABC view of our emotions, our responses (including anxiety, anger, or depression) to the behavior of a difficult person can be considered as:
   a. consequences of emotions and behavior.
   b. activating events.
   c. beliefs and self-talk.
   d. dispute and debate.

5.   Saying to yourself, "Others absolutely must give me what
     I want and must behave as I want, and if they don't, it's
     awful and I-can't-stand-it," is an example of:
     a. low frustration tolerance.
     b. irrational beliefs and self-talk.
     c. demandingness.
     d. all of the above are correct.

6.   The statement, "I dislike this person's behavior but I can
     stand it," is:
     a. coping self-talk.
     b. rational belief and self-talk.
     c. both of the above are correct.
     d. none of the above are correct.

7.   Guessing (silently, not out loud) at the irrational beliefs of
     your difficult person:
     a. is a waste of time.
     b. is even more upsetting.
     c. helps you to better understand your difficult person.
     d. is absurd.

8.   In coping with difficult people, all of the following are
     helpful except:
     a. changing one's anger to annoyance.
     b. expressing intense anger.
     c. expressing your annoyance but not your anger.
     d. being assertive in stating what you want, rather than
        being passive or aggressive.

9.   Which irrational belief causes procrastination?
     a. "This task will cause me too much frustration."
     b. "My emotional discomfort in doing this task will be too
        much to bear."
     c. "I shouldn't have to deal with this problem."
     d. all of the above cause procrastination.

10. An excuse which may keep me from studying SOS and
     practicing its principles is:
     a. believing there isn't much I can do about my anxiety,
        anger, or depression.
     b. "I don't have enough time to answer the questions and
        do the exercises."

    c. "My past history determines my present feelings and behavior."

    d. all of the above are excuses for not studying and practicing SOS principles.

11.   It's <u>unhealthy</u> to believe:

    a. "There will be periods of time when I will have reduced ability to manage my emotions."

    b. "I need to accept what I can't change."

    c. "I will try to deal with the world as it is and not as it absolutely must be."

    d. None of the above are unhealthy beliefs.

12.   People will be better adjusted if they:

    a. accept themselves.

    b. attempt to improve their self-esteem by performing better at tasks.

    c. express their anger and resentment rather than holding it in.

    d. work at improving their social skills.

13.   Instead of the irrational belief, "I must always succeed," a more sensible rational belief would be:

    a. "I should succeed."

    b. "Success is not important."

    c. "I won't think about success so much."

    d. "I prefer and want to succeed."

14.   In the following sentence, which word(s) need to be disputed? "I must be loved and approved by most all people significant to me."

    a. I

    b. must be

    c. loved and approved

    d. by most all people significant to me

15.   The core process that is central to emotional disturbance is:

    a. anger and low self-acceptance (LSA).

    b. low frustration tolerance (LFT).

    c. I-can't-stand-it-itis.

    d. demandingness and three major musts.

Answers to Part Four Questions:
1a 2b 3c 4a 5d 6c 7c 8b 9d 10d 11d 12a 13d 14b 15d

Part Four Exercises covering Chapters 10 & 11. Copy and complete.

Exercise A:
> Copy the "ABCDE Self-Analysis And Improvement Form." Select a recent situation (involving the behavior of a difficult person and yourself) with which you are upset and complete the entire form.

Exercise B:
> Turn to the following page. Answer the following five questions regarding "Pam's English Exam."

READ, STUDY, PRACTICE

(For Exercise B, "Pam's English Exam" – see the next page)

Pam's English Exam

Pam studies hard and receives a "D" on an English exam. After receiving the "D" Pam tells herself, "I must not have received a 'D' on that exam and because I did, I am a worthless person and will never do well in this English course. And I will probably never get my college degree." Pam leaves class feeling depressed, watches TV the rest of that day, and cuts all of her classes the following day.

1.   Pam thinks, "I must not have received..." and "I am a worthless person..." This is:
     a. an activating event.
     b. beliefs and self-talk.
     c. consequences, emotional or behavioral.
     d. dispute.

2.   Pam receives a "D" on the exam. This is:
     a. an activating event.
     b. beliefs and self-talk.
     c. consequences, emotional or behavioral.
     d. dispute.

3.   Pam thinks, "And I will probably never get my college degree." This is:
     a. an activating event.
     b. beliefs and self-talk.
     c. consequences, emotional or behavioral.
     d. dispute.

4.   Pam leaves class feeling depressed. This is:
     a. an activating event.
     b. beliefs and self-talk.
     c. consequences, emotional or behavioral.
     d. dispute.

5.   Pam watches TV the rest of that day, and cuts all of her classes the following day. This is:
     a. an activating event.
     b. beliefs and self-talk.
     c. consequences, emotional or behavioral.
     d. dispute.

Answers to the five questions involving Pam's English Exam:
1b   2a   3b   4c   5c

.

Chapter 13

Information For Counselors

ALBERT ELLIS EXPLAINING THE ABC's
TO PSYCHOLOGISTS – ROGERS, PERLS, AND FREUD

"To summarize, A activating events plus our B beliefs and self-talk largely cause our C consequences, emotions such as anxiety, anger, and depression and our behavior. This mainly explains the cause of our emotions and behavior, gentlemen!"

Technical talk: The chalkboard notations indicate: Beliefs are greater than Activating Events; Activating Events and Beliefs equal Consequences: Emotional & Behavioral; Dispute leads to Effects Of Dispute – New Emotions & Behavior. The concepts of Ego and Id have been dismissed. The seated individuals, from left to right, are Carl Rogers, Fritz Perls, and Sigmund Freud.

Albert Ellis gave his permission for this illustration to include himself. He also suggested that the concept A + B = C may be better illustrated by A x B = C.

Although this chapter is written primarily for the mental health professional, others also may find it interesting. It describes the goals of the *SOS Help For Emotions* program, suggests who may benefit from this program, and provides additional information about cognitive behavior therapy (CBT).

SOS and REBT emphasize the importance of the three major musts (demandingness) and five hot links (*condemnation & damnation, I-can't-stand-it-itis, awfulizing, I'm worthless*, and *always & never*) in the creation and continuation of emotional disturbance.*

Goals Of *SOS Help For Emotions*

We all face the unpleasant and unhealthy emotions of anxiety, anger, and depression. The primary goal of *SOS Help For Emotions: Managing Anxiety, Anger, And Depression* is to help people to better manage these emotions.

As a result of repeatedly applying SOS methods and principles, individuals are expected to more effectively handle life's problems and frustrations and to better manage relationships with others. They can set and attain more realistic goals, and achieve greater contentment as well.

SOS teaches principles and self-help methods from cognitive behavior therapy and especially from rational emotive behavior therapy (REBT).

---

* Technical Talk: The five hot connecting links are termed "irrational conclusions" or "derivatives from major musts" in rational emotive behavior therapy (Ellis, 1994). I prefer the term hot links, because they lead to hot, emotionally charged self-talk and unhealthy feelings. The hot links are in the order of CIA, IA.

The foundation for SOS is rational emotive behavior therapy and cognitive behavior therapy. References for over 500 outcome research studies on rational emotive behavior therapy are listed at <www.rebt.org>.

Who Can Benefit From SOS?

Both adults and teens can benefit from studying SOS. In cognitive behavior therapy, unlike other major approaches to therapy (for example, psychoanalytic, gestalt, client-centered, etc.), it's important that clients learn specific principles and self-help skills by reading, studying, and doing homework assignments.

SOS teaches valuable principles and methods used in cognitive behavior therapy. By recommending SOS, mental health professionals can more efficiently help their clients. Also, professionals who guide or counsel adults and youth, will find SOS an enjoyable, useful teaching tool.

Cognitive behavior therapy provides help in the form of individual therapy and counseling, group therapy, teaching youth the cause and control of their emotions, marriage and relationship counseling, alcohol and substance abuse counseling, anger management, and other programs teaching self-management of emotions and behavior.

SOS is intended for use in:
- public school programs and services
- clinics and counseling centers
- mental health centers
- hospitals
- treatment programs for anxiety, anger, or depression
- marriage and family counseling
- independent practice
- drug and alcohol treatment programs
- other mental health programs for youth and adults

College courses – SOS is often recommended as supplemental reading in such courses as:
- personality adjustment, theories of personality
- theory & methods of counseling & psychotherapy
- practicum in counseling & psychotherapy
- behavior therapy, behavior modification
- abnormal psychology, psychopathology
- other courses in human behavior

Using SOS In Counseling And Therapy

Client Homework Assignments And Quizzes

UNDERSTANDING OUR EMOTIONS
Chapter 1. Achieving Contentment And Our Goals
Chapter 2. ABC Origin Of Our Emotions And Behavior
Chapter 3. Self-Analysis Of Our ABC's
Quiz One And Exercises

MANAGING OUR EMOTIONS
Chapter 4. Managing Our Beliefs, Self-Talk, And
            Emotions
Chapter 5. Uprooting Our Irrational Beliefs And
            Self-Talk
Chapter 6. Common Irrational Beliefs And Self-Talk
Quiz Two And Exercises

MANAGING ANXIETY, ANGER, AND DEPRESSION
Chapter 7. Managing Anxiety
Chapter 8. Managing Anger
Chapter 9. Managing Depression
Quiz Three And Exercises

HELPING OURSELVES IN MORE WAYS
Chapter 10. Coping With Difficult People
Chapter 11. More Ways To Help Ourselves
Quiz Four And Exercises

Assign SOS chapters to clients as homework. Ask clients, after studying each two or three chapters, to take the quizzes and complete the exercises covering those chapters. See Chapter 12, Quizzes And Exercises.

To resolve emotional difficulties using REBT, clients need to complete the *ABCDE Self-Analysis And Improvement Form,* each day. This form was introduced in Chapter Five. An effective way for clients to learn this skill, is for the mental health professional and client to complete this form together several times. It's also important regularly to complete the *Daily Mood Record* (first presented in Chapter Three).

Cognitive Therapy Workshops
And Copyright Permission Information

Overhead transparencies and slides make workshops considerably more interesting for both professionals and clients.

Professionals who offer such workshops have permission to make overhead transparencies or PowerPoint slides (but not handouts or worksheets) of SOS illustrations and boxes as long as only one copy is made of any illustration or box and the following copyright and permission notice is visible on <u>each</u> overhead or PowerPoint slide. This notice must read: "© 2002 by Lynn Clark. Illustration is from *SOS Help For Emotions* and used by permission."

An example of a copyright and permission notice to be placed on each overhead or slide is given below.

> "© 2002 by Lynn Clark. Illustration is from *SOS Help For Emotions* and used by permission."

You need to obtain written permission from SOS Programs & Parents Press to use illustrations or boxes in handouts, worksheets, or in any form other than overheads and PowerPoint slides.

Cognitive Behavior Therapies

The term cognitive therapy has two meanings, one narrow and one broad. Cognitive therapy in the narrow sense refers to the particular approach to therapy developed by Aaron Beck.

In the broader meaning, cognitive therapy or the cognitive therapies refer to those therapy approaches, methods, and therapists (for example, Ellis, Beck, Meichenbaum, Burns) emphasizing the importance of cognitions in determining emotion and behavior.

The following are the three major cognitive therapy or cognitive behavior therapy systems, depending on the term that you prefer.
  • Rational Emotive Behavior Therapy (REBT – Ellis)
  • Cognitive Therapy (CT – Beck)
  • Cognitive Behavior Modification (CBM – Meichenbaum)

There are many similarities and some differences between the above therapy systems. The three approaches borrow concepts and therapy techniques from each other. The two most influential approaches are REBT and CT.

Rational emotive behavior therapy (REBT) was originated by Dr. Albert Ellis in the 1950's. Contemporary therapists consider Ellis to be the grandfather of cognitive behavior therapy (Corey, 1996).

Aaron Beck, like Ellis, was originally trained in psychoanalysis, but also found it insufficient as a method for helping clients. Beck started developing his system, now called cognitive therapy (CT), in the early 1960's.

Donald Meichenbaum began developing cognitive behavior modification (CBM) in the 1970's. More eclectic, Meichenbaum has focused on treatment for posttraumatic stress disorder in recent years.

Several important distinctions exist between REBT therapists and other cognitive behavior therapists (including CT cognitive therapy). One major difference is that REBT assumes *demandingness of the client (e.g., major musts)* as a core cause of distress, and helps the client to dispute this demandingness. The other cognitive behavior therapists don't make this assumption and consequently don't help the client to dispute it.*

See the text by Corey (2000), *Theory And Practice Of Counseling And Psychotherapy* which compares and contrasts these related cognitive behavior therapy approaches.

Professional Training And Materials
For Rational Emotive Behavior Therapy (REBT)

Albert Ellis Institute Of Rational Emotive Behavior Therapy, in New York City, offers various levels of REBT clinical training for mental health professionals. Professional workshops, offered periodically, also are given in various cities in the United States. Affiliated branches of REBT may be found in foreign countries. The Institute's catalog and website describe training opportunities for professionals.

The Institute offers professional books and videotapes as well as self-help books and materials. Ask for a catalog.

Albert Ellis Institute For Rational Emotive Behavior Therapy, 45 East 65th Street, New York, NY 10021. Telephone is (212)535-0822 or (800)323-4738. The website is <http://www.rebt.org>

REBT therapy sessions (actual sessions, not role-played) are available on videotape for mental health professionals ordering on a professional letterhead. Tapes of more than ten therapy sessions, each lasting from 38 to 55 minutes, are available. The therapy interviews are conducted by Albert Ellis, Ray DiGiuseppe, Dominic DiMattia, Janet Wolfe, and other REBT therapists. Of course, the clients gave permission for the sessions to be videotaped and made available for training professionals.

---

* Personal communication with Don Beal.

This particular series of tapes, beginning in the mid 1990's, provides captions superimposed on live action, along with brief comments by therapists which help the viewer to follow the steps of therapy. The therapy steps described in *A Primer On Rational-Emotive Therapy* (Dryden & DiGiuseppe, 1990) correspond to the steps, captions, and comments on the videotapes and are a useful learning aid. The *Primer* as well as the videotapes may be ordered from Albert Ellis Institute.

Few videotaped psychotherapy interviews which are conducted by female therapists are available for training purposes. The REBT therapy interviews conducted by Janet Wolfe are unique in this respect.   My graduate students, both male and female, have especially enjoyed observing Dr. Wolfe counsel clients.

REBT books I recommend for therapists include the following. They are all available from Albert Ellis Institute.

Dryden, W. & DiGiuseppe, R. (1990). *A Primer On Rational-Emotive Therapy.* Champaign, IL: Research Press. Consider also ordering the REBT video interviews described above.

Dryden, W. & Neenan, M. (1994). *Dictionary Of Rational Emotive Behaviour Therapy.* London: Whurr Publishers. This book is more than a dictionary and is interesting reading for therapists.

Ellis, A. (1998). *How to Control Your Anxiety before It Controls You.* New York: Citadel Press.

Ellis, A. (1994). *Reason And Emotion In Psychotherapy.* (2nd ed.). New York: Birch Lane Press of Carol Publishing Group.

Bernard, M. & Wolfe, J. (Eds.). (2000). *The REBT Resource Book For Practitioners*, 2nd ed. New York: Albert Ellis Institute For Rational Emotive Behavior Therapy.

Walen, S., DiGiuseppe, R., & Dryden, W. (1992). *A Practitioner's Guide To Rational-Emotive Therapy.* (2nd ed.). NY: Oxford University Press.

Information about cognitive therapy professional training and materials is available from The Beck Institute. The address is, The Beck Institute For Cognitive Therapy And Research, GSB Building, City Line and Belmont Avenues, Suite 700, Bala Cynwyd, PA 19004-1610. The telephone is (610)644-3020 and the website is <http://www.beckinstitute.org>

David Burns, author of *Feeling Good: The New Mood Therapy*, offers highly rated cognitive behavior therapy workshops in various cities for mental health professionals. See <http://www.feelinggood.com>

The cognitive behavior therapies are a valuable approach to self-help and offer an effective way to assist both adults and youth. Cognitive behavior therapy is becoming increasingly important due to the emphasis on briefer therapy and on research-validated treatment methods.

The media is giving extensive attention to cognitive behavior therapy and its methods as applied to a wide range of emotional problems and disorders.

Sigmund Freud (1856 - 1939) is the founder of psychoanalysis. My family and I visited his office (now a museum of psychoanalysis) in Vienna, Austria, where he practiced therapy for over 25 years.

Albert Ellis (1913 -) was originally trained as a psychoanalyst, but departed from this approach for helping people. He is known as the father of rational emotive behavior therapy and grandfather of cognitive behavior therapy. Ellis is the first therapist to emphasize the role that self-talk and beliefs play in shaping our emotions, emotional problems, and emotional disorders.

REFERENCES

Alberti, R. & Emmons, M. (2001). *Your perfect right. 8th ed.* San Luis Obispo, CA: Impact Publishers.

American Psychiatric Association. (2000). *Diagnostic and statistical manual of mental disorders, Fourth Edition, Text Revision.* Washington, DC: American Psychiatric Press.

American Psychiatric Association. (1994). *American psychiatric glossary.* Washington, DC: American Psychiatric Press.

Beal, D., Kopec, A. M., & DiGiuseppe, R. (1996). Disputing clients' irrational beliefs. *Journal of Rational-Emotive & Cognitive Behavior Therapy*, 14, 215-229.

Beck, A. T., & Emery, G. (1985) *Anxiety disorders and phobias: A cognitive perspective.* New York: Basic Books.

Beck, A. & Rush, J. (1995). Cognitive therapy. In H. Kaplan & B. Sadock (Eds.), *Comprehensive textbook of psychiatry, VI*, (pp. 1847-1850). Baltimore: Williams & Wilkins.

Beckfield, D. (1994). *Master your panic and take back your life.* San Luis Obispo, CA: Impact Publishers.

Bernard, M. & Wolfe, J. (Eds.). (1993). *The RET resource book for practitioners.* New York: Albert Ellis Institute For Rational Emotive Therapy.

Bernard, M. & Wolfe, J. (Eds.). (2000). *The REBT resource book for practitioners, 2nd ed.* New York: Albert Ellis Institute For Rational Emotive Therapy.

Bolles, R. (2001). *What color is your parachute?* Berkeley, CA: Ten Speed Press.

Bolton, R. (1979). *People skills.* New York: Touchstone.

Borcherdt, B. (1989). *Think straight! Feel great.* Sarasota, FL: Professional Resource Exchange.

Bramson, R. (1981). *Coping with difficult people.* New York: Ballantine.

Burns, D. (1999). *Feeling good: The new mood therapy.* New York: Avon Books.

Burns, D. (1999). *The feeling good handbook.* New York: Plume.

Carnegie, D. (1998). *How to win friends and influence people. Rev. ed.* New York: Pocket Books.

Clark, L. (1996 with 2003 Revisions). *SOS help for parents: A practical guide for handling common everyday behavior problems. 2nd. ed.* Bowling Green, KY: SOS Programs & Parents Press.

Clark, L. F. & Neuringer, C. (1971). Repressor-Sensitizer personality styles and associated levels of verbal ability, social intelligence, sex knowledge, and quantitative ability. *Journal of Consulting and Clinical Psychology, 36*, 183-188.

Corey G. (2000). *Theory and practice of counseling and psychotherapy.* 5th ed. Wadsworth Publishing.

DiGiuseppe, R. (1989). *What Shall I Do With My Anger: Hold It In Or Let It Out?* [Audiotape]. New York: Albert Ellis Institute For Rational Emotive Therapy.

DiGiuseppe, R., Tafrate, R., & Eckhardt, C. (1994). Critical issues in the treatment of anger. *Cognitive And Behavioral Practice, 1*,111-132.

Dinkmeyer, D. & McKay, G. (1998). *Parenting teenagers: Systematic training for effective parenting of teens.* Circle Pines, MN: American Guidance Service.

Dryden, W. (1990). *Dealing with anger problems: Rational-emotive therapeutic interventions.* Sarasota, FL: Professional Resource Exchange.

Dryden, W. & DiGiuseppe, R. (1990). *A primer on rational-emotive Therapy.* Champaign, IL: Research Press. Available from Albert Ellis Institute For Rational Emotive Therapy.

Dryden, W. & Neenan, M. (1994). *Dictionary of rational emotive behaviour therapy.* London: Whurr Publishers. Available from Albert Ellis Institute For Rational Emotive Therapy.

Covey, S. (1989). *The 7 habits of effective people.* New York: Simon & Schuster.

Ellis, A. (2001, June). General session. REBT/CBT Conference, Keystone, Colorado.

Ellis, A. (1998). *How to control your anxiety before it controls you.* New York: Citadel Press.

Ellis, A. (1991). *Dealing With Difficult People* [Audiotape]. New York: Albert Ellis Institute For Rational Emotive Therapy.

Ellis, A. (1994). *Reason and emotion in psychotherapy.* 2nd ed. New York, NY: Birch Lane Press of Carol Publishing Group. Available from Albert Ellis Institute For Rational Emotive Therapy.

Ellis, A. (1992). *How to stubbornly refuse to make yourself miserable about anything — Yes Anything!* Secaucus, NJ: Lyle Stuart.

Ellis, A. (date not known). *Conquering Low Frustration Tolerance* [Audiotape]. New York: Albert Ellis Institute For Rational Emotive Therapy.

Ellis, A. & Harper, R. A. (1997). *A guide to rational living.* Rev. ed.

North Hollywood, CA: Wilshire Publishing.
Ellis, A. & Lang, A. (1994). *How to keep people from pushing your buttons.* New York, NY: Birch Lane Press of Carol Publishing Group. Available from Albert Ellis Institute For Rational Emotive Therapy.
Ellis, A. & Tafrate, R. C. (1997), *How to control your anger before it controls you.* Secauscus, NJ: Birch Lane Press.
Faber, A. & Mazlish, E. (1999). *How to talk so kids will listen & listen so kids will talk.* New York: Avon.
Gatchel, R. & Blanchard, E. (Eds.). (1993). *Psychophysiological disorders: Research and clinical applications.* Washington, DC: American Psychological Association.
Gold, M. (1989). *The good news about panic, anxiety, and phobias.* New York, NY: Bantam Books.
Goleman, D. (1995). *Emotional intelligence.* New York: Bantam Books.
Goleman, D. (1998). *Working with emotional intelligence.* New York: Bantam Books.
Hales, D. & Hales, R. (1996). *Caring for the mind: The comprehensive guide to mental health.* New York: Bantam.
Kopec, A. M., Beal, D., & DiGiuseppe, R. (1994). Training in RET: Disputational strategies. *Journal of Rational-Emotive & Cognitive Behavior Therapy,* 12, 47-60.
Merriam-Webster's collegiate dictionary. (10th ed.). (1996). Springfield, MA: Merriam-Webster Incorporated.
Nielsen, S., Johnson, W., & Ellis, A. (2001). *Counseling and Psychotherapy With Religious Persons: A Rational Emotive Behavior Therapy Approach.* Mahwah, New Jersey: Lawrence Erlbaum Associates.
Neal, F., Davison, G., & Haaga, D. (1995). *Exploring abnormal psychology.* New York: John Wiley & Sons.
Norcross, J., Santrock, J., Campbell, L., Smith, T., Sommer, R., & Zukerman, E. (2000). *The authoritative guide to self-help resources in mental health.* New York: Guilford Press.
Nottingham, E. (2001). *It's not as bad as it seems.* Writer's Club Press.
Schaefer, C. (1994). *How to talk to your kids about really important things: For children four to twelve.* San Francisco, CA: Jossey-Bass Publishers.
Schaefer, C. (1999). *How to talk to teens about really important things: Specific questions and answers and useful things to say.* San Francisco, CA: Jossey-Bass Publishers.

Tannen, D. (1990). *You just don't understand: Women and men in conversation.* New York: Ballantine.

Walen, S., DiGiuseppe, R., & Dryden, W. (1992). *A practitioner's guide to rational-emotive therapy.* (2nd ed.). NY: Oxford University Press.

Warren, R. & Zgourides, G. (1991). *Anxiety disorders: A rational-emotive perspective.* New York: Pergamon Press (now Longwood Division of Allyn & Bacon).

Weinrach, S. (1996). Nine experts describe the essence of rational-emotive therapy while standing on one foot. *Journal of Counseling & Development,* 74, 326-331.

Wilson, G., Nathan, P., O'Leary, K., & Clark, Lee. (1995). *Abnormal psychology: Integrating perspectives.* Boston: Allyn & Bacon.

Wolfe, J. (1992). *What to do when he has a headache.* New York: Hyperion. Available from Albert Ellis Institute For Rational Emotive Therapy.

The foundation for SOS is rational emotive behavior therapy and cognitive behavior therapy. References for over 500 outcome research studies on rational emotive behavior therapy are listed at <www.rebt.org>.

Index

Author Index

Index

General Index

For some terms such as "anxiety," the references are too numerous to list. In those cases, only the most important references to the term are noted. Page numbers are noted for some illustrations. Refer to the Author Index for references to names.

SOS Parenting Program

SOS Help For Parents Book
The Video SOS Help For Parents

SCENE FROM THE SOS VIDEO

"Thanks for tying your sister's shoe!"

SOS Help For Parents is a book and video-based parent education program which helps children, ages two to twelve, improve their behavior and emotional adjustment. It is internationally recommended and used by psychologists, pediatricians, child psychiatrists, teachers, and other professionals, as well as parents. SOS teaches over 20 methods for helping children and offers the most complete instructions available for using time-out.

"The multi-media approach [of the SOS Help For Parents Program] makes the information accessible to parents and children at all levels of adjustment and functioning."
– Journal of Marital And Family Therapy

SOS Help For Parents: A Practical Guide For Handling Common Everyday Behavior Problems

English SOS

Spanish SOS

Turkish SOS

Chinese SOS
Beijing Normal University

Korean SOS

Chinese SOS
Taiwan

Hungarian SOS

Arabic SOS

Icelandic SOS

The goal of SOS is to help parents to be better parents, by improving their behavior management skills. Professionals who educate parents, counsel parents, or render services to children and families will find the SOS book and SOS Video useful educational and counseling tools. With over 100 illustrations, the *SOS Help For Parents* book is both enjoyable to read and easy to understand.

Visit our website and learn how you can use *The SOS Video* to educate or counsel parents in behavior management. Download complimentary educational materials. Also, see video and audio clips in English and Spanish at http://**www.sosprograms.com**

The Video SOS Help For Parents

The SOS Video program is used by counselors, clinics, child treatment programs, parent groups, educators, places of worship, day-care centers, Head Start centers, social service professionals and in college classes. *The SOS Video* program is intended for behavior management workshops, staff development, in-service training, teacher training, and for use in college classes.

The *Video Leader's Guide* gives guidelines for presenting the program. Part One of the video may be viewed individually or with a group.

For Part Two, a discussion leader needs to guide the discussion following each of the 43 parenting scenes. The *Video Leader's Guide* offers discussion questions and answers for each scene. Discussion questions and answers for two sample parenting scenes are presented on the following pages. Each participant receives a Parent Handout sheet listing 20 parenting rules, common errors, and methods for managing behavior. Using this Parent Handout, participants are asked to identify which of these parenting rules and methods a scene demonstrates. This teaching method provides the discussion leader with immediate feedback on how much the participants are learning. Allow about three sessions to present the complete video-based program. The program includes the 72 minute DVD (plays internationally), 72 minute VHS (identical content), Video Leader's Guide, parent handouts, and Child Management Skills Test (CMST).

Technical Talk: The approach of the SOS behavior management and parenting program includes principles of learning and reinforcement, social learning, humanistic-Adlerian psychology, and reflective listening applied to helping children. The program, based on the book *SOS Help For Parents*, is practical, clear, easy to understand, and rests on data-based research studies of behavior change. This video-based program, however, is easy to lead and does not require professional training.

SOS Video Scene #17
from Video Leader's Guide

REFUSING APPLE JUICE

Rule #3 Correct some bad behavior (but use mild correction only.)

The bad behavior is knocking the glass of water off the table and loss of self-control.

The mild correction is time-out. Mother provides an example of a "good command" in sending her son to time-out.

Script:

Mother brings apple juice and two crackers to Mitchell who is sitting at the table and demanding cookies.

Mitchell: *"No! I want those cookies!"*

Mom: *"You can have the crackers and apple juice to hold you over to dinner time. It will be ready in about 30 minutes and you may have cookies for dessert."*

Mitchell: *"I don't want any dumb juice!"* (Said as he knocks the glass off the table.)

Mom: *"Time-out! You knocked the glass over. Go now!"*

Mitchell: *"I don't want time-out! I want those cookies!"* (Said as he stomps off to time-out)

Questions, Answers, And Comments:

Q: Which rule or error did mother follow?

A: Rule #3 Correct some bad behavior (but use mild correction only).

Q: What is the bad behavior?

A: Knocking the glass over.

Q: What is the correction?

A: Time-out.

Q: When frustrated in the future, is the child more or less likely to lose control?

A: Less likely.

Q: Did mother use time-out correctly?

A: Yes. SOS recommends sending a child to time-out within 10 seconds following the bad behavior and using 10 words or less. Mother sent him to time-out immediately and used only 8 words. Also, mother gave a "good command" in sending her son to time-out.

Suggestions to Presenter: Save a long discussion on time-out until after this video program, and then offer training on time-out.

Technical comments:

Scene demonstrates mild correction of undesirable behavior using time-out. A "good command" is used in sending the child to time-out.

SOS Video Scene #18
from Video Leader's Guide

SWEEPING THE WALK

Rule #1 Reward good behavior (and do it quickly and often).
 The good behavior is trying to help with work.
 The reward is a social reward (descriptive praise).
 This is also an example of mother setting a good example and daughter imitating mother's behavior.

Script:
 Mother and daughter are sweeping the walk in front of their house.

 Mom: *"Nicole, I sure like it when you help Mommy sweep the walk. You're doing a good job!"*
 Nicole: (Child doesn't say anything, but continues working hard sweeping the walk.)

Questions, Answers, And Comments:
Q: Which rule or error did mother follow?
 A: Rule #1 Reward good behavior (and do it quickly and often).
Q: What is the good behavior?
 A: Helping mother with work, sweeping the walk.
Q: What is the reward?
 A: A social reward (descriptive praise).
Q: Is the child more or less likely to help mother in the future?
 A: More likely.
Q: What kind of social rewards did mother use?
 A: Smiles, attention, and praise (descriptive praise).

Point To Make: Little Nicole doesn't have to do a perfect job to earn her mother's praise. Parents should reward <u>attempts</u> to do a chore. Also, mother is being a good role-model and Nicole is imitating mother's behavior. Most of what children learn is by observing their parents and others.

Technical Comments:
 Scene illustrates positive reinforcement of daughter's desirable behavior, with a social reinforcer (descriptive praise). Scene also demonstrates social imitation (daughter is imitating mother's behavior) and shaping (rewarding an attempt to sweep the walk).

The Video
SOS
Help For Parents
A Video-Discussion

Parent Education

& Counseling Program

See video clips at <http://**www.sosprograms.com**>

This video parent education and counseling program is based on the book, *SOS Help For Parents* and includes the 72 minute DVD (plays internationally, region free), 72 minute videocassette (identical content), *Video Leader's Guide*, reproducible *Parent Handouts*, *SOS Help For Parents* book, and *Child Management Skills Test* (CMST).

The *SOS Video* program is used by counselors, parent groups, educators, places of worship, and social service professionals. It is intended for parenting workshops, staff development, in-service training, teacher training, parent counseling, and in college classrooms.

Part One may be viewed by a group or an individual. For Part Two, a discussion leader should guide the discussion following each of the parenting scenes. The easy-to-use *Video Leader's Guide* offers discussion questions and answers for each scene. Enjoyable and user-friendly, *The SOS Video* program educates participants in more than 20 behavior management skills. Over 10,000 SOS Video programs are in use.

El Video SOS Ayuda Para Padres

This easy to teach program includes the 72 minute DVD (plays internationally, region free), 72 minute videocassette (identical content), *Video Leader's Guide*, reproducible *Parent Handouts* in Spanish, and *SOS Ayuda Para Padres* book. See a sample Spanish video clip at <http://**www.sosprograms.com**>

"How To Use Time-Out Effectively"
Audio Program (67 minutes).

This audio program demonstrates and teaches time-out skills. You'll hear answers to common time-out questions and learn to avoid nine common time-out mistakes. Todd (age nine) and Lisa (age eleven) tell how they feel about time-out. For individual listening, group listening, and behavior management workshops. Includes *Time-Out Guide*, illustrated *Time-Out Chart*, CD, & audiotape (identical content as CD).

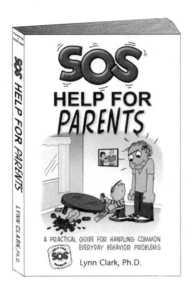

SOS Help For Parents:
A Practical Guide For Handling Common Everyday Behavior Problems

- Will make your life more enjoyable
- Will make your life less stressful
- Over 240 pages with 100 illustrations
- Over 20 methods for managing difficult behavior
- Easy to understand and apply

What Others Are Saying About SOS

"SOS turned our family around...I really regained my self-confidence as a parent."
— Mother of two, Riverview, Michigan

"Lynn Clark...drew from his 20 years of working with parents and children when he wrote SOS Help For Parents."
— USA Today

"SOS is an extremely comprehensive book...an excellent book. We highly recommend it."
— Journal of Child Clinical Psychology

Visit our website at
http://**www.sosprograms.com**
See video and audio clips.

ORDER FORM

SOS Programs & Parents Press, PO Box 2180,
Bowling Green, KY 42102-2180 USA

You also can order at our website. Order by phone 1-800-576-1582 toll free, weekdays, 9:00am to 3:00pm Central Standard Time. Can phone 1-270-842-4571. FAX is 270-796-9194. Bookstores can order from Ingram and Baker & Taylor.

For VISA or MasterCard orders, clearly indicate which card, card expiration date, card #, and phone #.

____ Copies of **SOS Help For Emotions** book for $14.00. In English only. Not a parenting book. (2nd Edition Book ISBN-10: 0-935111-52-2 and ISBN-13: 978-0-935111-52-1)

____ Copies of **SOS Help For Parents** book in English for $14.00. For parents of children 2 to 12 years old. In English. (3nd Edition Book ISBN-10: 0-935111-21-2 and ISBN-13: 978-0935111-21-7)

____ Copies of Spanish book **SOS Ayuda Para Padres** for $14.00. For parents of children 2 to 12 years old. (Spanish Book ISBN-10: 0-935111-47-6 and ISBN-13: 978-0-935111-47-7)

____ Copies of **"How To Use Time-Out Effectively"** audio program (67 minutes), Time-Out Guide, Time-Out Chart, CD & audiotape for $14.00. For parents and parent workshops. (Audio ISBN 0-935111-32-8)

____ **Free DVD SOS Sampler–Preview Video** on DVD (8 minutes long) to professionals & educators, in English only. Includes sample parent handouts and discussion guides for two scenes. Free shipping.

____ **The DVD Video SOS Help For Parents** education program for $180.00, shipping within USA included. Program includes 72 minute DVD (plays in all regions of the world) and 72 minute VHS (identical content), Video Leader's Guide, Parent Handouts, SOS Help For Parents book, and other materials. (SOS DVD Video ISBN-10: 0-935111-38-7 and ISBN-13: 978-0-935111-38-5) Visit our website and see video samples. See description on other pages.

____ **El DVD Video SOS Ayuda Para Padres** education program for $180.00, shipping within USA included. Includes 72 minute DVD (plays in all regions of the world) & 72 minute VHS (identical content), Video Leader's Guide, SOS Ayuda Para Padres book, and Spanish handouts, (Spanish ISBN-10: 0-935111-48-4 and ISBN-13: 978-0-935111-48-4) Visit our website and see a two minute video sample in Spanish.

ORDER FORM Continued

You also can order at our website. Orders from individuals must be prepaid by check or credit card. Agencies may FAX their purchase orders. We pay any taxes. Federal Tax #61-1225614. Bookstores can order from Ingram and Baker & Taylor.

   If not satisfied, I understand that I may return any of the materials for a refund.

Mailing Label — Please Clearly Print

Name: _____

Address: _____

City: _____ State: _____ Zip: _____

Credit Card Check One: ☐ VISA   ☐ MasterCard

Credit card Expiration Date _____

Account # _____

_____
         Print name as it appears on card.

Daytime Phone (_____) _____
            (Telephone number is necessary if credit card is used.)

Shipping*:* Include $5.00 shipping for first book or audiotape and $1.00 shipping for each additional book or audiotape.

_____ ***Air Mail or UPS:*** I can't wait 2 weeks for Book Rate shipping. Enclosed is $6.00 total shipping for first book or audiotape, and $1.00 for each additional book or audiotape for Air Mail or UPS.

_____ ***Quantity Discounts:*** If you are ordering at least five books, deduct 20% from the cost of the books. You may mix titles of books to total five.

_____ I am a counselor, educator, or professional.

_____ See our website at http://**www.sosprograms.com**

Foreign Orders must be prepaid in US funds (credit cards or checks on US banks). For shipping, first book is $12 and each additional book is $2. Also, English and foreign edition books are available through Amazon. Email questions to sos@sosprograms.com

Call for availability of foreign editions of SOS Help For Parents. All foreign editions, when available, are $14.00.

Visit our website at
http://**www.sosprograms.com**
See video and audio clips.

ORDER FORM

SOS Programs & Parents Press, PO Box 2180,
Bowling Green, KY 42102-2180 USA

You also can order at our website. Order by phone 1-800-576-1582 toll free, weekdays, 9:00am to 3:00pm Central Standard Time. Can phone 1-270-842-4571. FAX is 270-796-9194. Bookstores can order from Ingram and Baker & Taylor.

For VISA or MasterCard orders, clearly indicate which card, card expiration date, card #, and phone #.

____ Copies of **SOS Help For Emotions** book for $14.00. In English only. Not a parenting book. (2nd Edition Book ISBN-10: 0-935111-52-2 and ISBN-13: 978-0-935111-52-1)

____ Copies of **SOS Help For Parents** book in English for $14.00. For parents of children 2 to 12 years old. In English. (3nd Edition Book ISBN-10: 0-935111-21-2 and ISBN-13: 978-0935111-21-7)

____ Copies of Spanish book **SOS Ayuda Para Padres** for $14.00. For parents of children 2 to 12 years old. (Spanish Book ISBN-10: 0-935111-47-6 and ISBN-13: 978-0-935111-47-7)

____ Copies of **"How To Use Time-Out Effectively"** audio program (67 minutes), Time-Out Guide, Time-Out Chart, CD & audiotape for $14.00. For parents and parent workshops. (Audio ISBN 0-935111-32-8)

____ **Free DVD SOS Sampler–Preview Video** on DVD (8 minutes long) to professionals & educators, in English only. Includes sample parent handouts and discussion guides for two scenes. Free shipping.

____ **The DVD Video SOS Help For Parents** education program for $180.00, shipping within USA included. Program includes 72 minute DVD (plays in all regions of the world) and 72 minute VHS (identical content), Video Leader's Guide, Parent Handouts, SOS Help For Parents book, and other materials. (SOS DVD Video ISBN-10: 0-935111-38-7 and ISBN-13: 978-0-935111-38-5) Visit our website and see video samples. See description on other pages.

____ **El DVD Video SOS Ayuda Para Padres** education program for $180.00, shipping within USA included. Includes 72 minute DVD (plays in all regions of the world) & 72 minute VHS (identical content), Video Leader's Guide, SOS Ayuda Para Padres book, and Spanish handouts, (Spanish ISBN-10: 0-935111-48-4 and ISBN-13: 978-0-935111-48-4) Visit our website and see a two minute video sample in Spanish.

ORDER FORM Continued

You also can order at our website. Orders from individuals must be prepaid by check or credit card. Agencies may FAX their purchase orders. We pay any taxes. Federal Tax #61-1225614. Bookstores can order from Ingram and Baker & Taylor.

If not satisfied, I understand that I may return any of the materials for a refund.

Mailing Label — Please Clearly Print

Name: _____

Address: _____

City: _____ State: _____ Zip: _____

Credit Card Check One: ☐ VISA   ☐ MasterCard

Credit card Expiration Date _____

Account # _____

_____
Print name as it appears on card.

Daytime Phone (_____) _____
(Telephone number is necessary if credit card is used.)

Shipping: Include $5.00 shipping for first book or audiotape and $1.00 shipping for each additional book or audiotape.

____ *Air Mail or UPS:* I can't wait 2 weeks for Book Rate shipping. Enclosed is $6.00 total shipping for first book or audiotape, and $1.00 for each additional book or audiotape for Air Mail or UPS.

____ *Quantity Discounts:* If you are ordering at least five books, deduct 20% from the cost of the books. You may mix titles of books to total five.

____ I am a counselor, educator, or professional.

____ See our website at http://**www.sosprograms.com**

Foreign Orders must be prepaid in US funds (credit cards or checks on US banks). For shipping, first book is $12 and each additional book is $2. Also, English and foreign edition books are available through Amazon. Email questions to sos@sosprograms.com

Call for availability of foreign editions of SOS Help For Parents. All foreign editions, when available, are $14.00.

A HOLE IN THE SIDEWALK
Autobiography In Five Short Chapters

Chapter One
I walk down the street.
There is a deep hole in the sidewalk.
I fall in. I am lost....I am helpless. It isn't my fault.
It takes forever to find a way out.

Chapter Two
I walk down the same street.
There is a deep hole in the sidewalk.
I pretend I don't see it.
I fall in again. I can't believe I am in the same place.
But it isn't my fault. It still takes a long time to get out.

Chapter Three
I walk down the same street.
There is a deep hole in the sidewalk.
I see it is there.
I still fall in...it's a habit...but,
My eyes are open. I know where I am.
It is my fault. I get out immediately.

Chapter Four
I walk down the same street.
There is a deep hole in the sidewalk.
I walk around it.

Chapter Five
I walk down another street.